Flanagan, John Theodore
     Profile of Vachel Lindsay

Profile
of
Vachel Lindsay

Compiled by
John T. Flanagan
University of Illinois

Charles E. Merrill Publishing Company
A Bell & Howell Company
Columbus, Ohio

CHARLES E. MERRILL PROFILES

Under the General Editorship of
Matthew J. Bruccoli and Joseph Katz

Copyright © 1970 by Charles E. Merrill Publishing Company, Columbus, Ohio. All rights reserved. No part of this book may be reproduced in any form, electronic or mechanical, including photocopy, recording, or any information storage and retrieval system without permission in writing from the publisher.

ISBN: 0-675-09287-6

Library of Congress Catalog Number: 79-130279

1 2 3 4 5 6 7 8 9 — 79 78 76 75 74 73 72 71 70

Printed in the United States of America

Preface

Vachel Lindsay's celebrity began with the publication in *Poetry* in January, 1913, of "General William Booth Enters Into Heaven." For the next decade he continued to produce the staccato, highly cadenced verse ("The Congo," "The Santa Fe Trail," "The Kallyope Yell") which became his trademark and which explained his tremendous appeal on the lecture platform. The appearance of *The Congo and Other Poems* in 1914 attracted wide attention; this and subsequent books elicited estimates and evaluations from most of the literary critics of the 1920's. In addition to the writers represented in the present collection, T. K. Whipple, Llewellyn Jones, Floyd Dell, Alfred Kreymborg, Marianne Moore, Clement Wood, and Louis Untermeyer wrote appreciations of Lindsay's work, some of their criticism being astringent but most of it laudatory.

After Lindsay's death in 1931 there was a flutter of obituary estimates. Two books about the poet had preceded his death: Stephen Graham's *Tramping With a Poet in the Rockies*, 1922, and Albert E. Trombly's *Vachel Lindsay, Adventurer*, 1929. In 1935 Edgar Lee Masters published his *Vachel Lindsay: A Poet in America*, a volume which is evasive and sometimes inaccurate in biographical detail but which provides substantial criticism. Mark Harris's *City of Discontent*, 1952, is a fictionalized biography of Lindsay, and Eleanor Ruggles's *The West-Going Heart*, 1959, is the most reliable and complete factual account of Lindsay's life but is unimportant as criticism. In 1970 Ann Massa, an English specialist in American civilization, published *Vachel Lindsay, Fieldworker for the American Dream*, an examination of Lindsay's ideas as revealed in both poetry and prose which is not always successful in attempting to present him as a coherent thinker. In the *Baylor Bulletin* for September, 1940 (Volume XLIII, pp. 1-121), A. Joseph Armstrong published *Letters of Nicholas Vachel Lindsay to A. Joseph Armstrong*, an interesting revelation of Lindsay as an indefatigable correspondent. Mark Harris edited the *Selected Poems of Vachel Lindsay* in 1963 and wrote an appreciative but uncritical introduction to the volume. As late as 1966 only five doctoral dissertations had been written on Lindsay's work; they remain unpublished.

The following essays dealing with the life and work of Lindsay have been arranged to represent three approaches to the subject: contemporary estimates, in some cases the work of those who knew the poet personally; comprehensive evaluations stimulated by his death and the need to come to some kind of decision about his significance as a writer and cultural phenomenon; and more specialized examinations of particular aspects of Lindsay's work. Thus the essays by Harriet Monroe, who encouraged the young poet by welcoming his verse to *Poetry*, Conrad Aiken, Herbert S. Gorman, Carl Van Doren, and Albert Edmund Trombly represent the reactions of critics writing when Vachel Lindsay was a new star on the poetic horizon and seemed a living, dynamic force. The longer articles by Hazelton Spencer, Henry Morton Robinson, W. R. Moses, and Edgar Lee Masters (the last a kind of capsule preview of his biography) illustrate the attitudes of critics at the time of Lindsay's death. Henry Seidel Canby's obituary editorial in the *Saturday Review of Literature* belongs to this same period. Later evaluations by Nils Erik Enkvist and Austin Warren suggest the need for evaluating Lindsay's poetry from special points of view and deal perceptively with his use of folklore and his command of poetic technique and diction. The reminiscent article by William Rose Benét, himself a poet as well as a critic, gives unusual insight into Lindsay's personality and provides fragments of his correspondence. Finally I have included my own appraisal of Lindsay in order to present an essay from the decade of the 1960's.

JOHN T. FLANAGAN

Urbana, Illinois, May 1, 1970

Contents

Chronicle of Events

1879   (Nicholas) Vachel Lindsay born on November 10, Springfield, Illinois, the son of Dr. Vachel Thomas and Esther Catharine Frazee Lindsay.

1897   Graduated Springfield High School.

1897-1900   Hiram College, Hiram, Ohio.

1901-1903   Student at the Art Institute of Chicago.

1903-1905   Student at New York School of Art. Also tried drawing and writing poetry.

1906   Walking trip from Florida to Kentucky. June-September, European trip with his parents.

1907   Metropolitan Museum guide and YMCA lecturer in New York City.

1908   Walking trip from New York City to Hiram, Ohio.

1908-1912   Residence in the family home at Springfield, writing verse, compiling *The Village Magazine*, contributing poems to such magazines as *The Independent* and *The American Magazine* as well as to the *Illinois State Register* in Springfield.

1913   "General William Booth Enters into Heaven" appeared in January in *Poetry: A Magazine of Verse*, his first popular success. First collection of poems published, *General William Booth Enters into Heaven and Other Poems*.

1914   Recited "The Congo" in Springfield and Chicago. Published *The Congo and Other Poems* and a chronicle of his walking tours, *Adventures While Preaching the Gospel of Beauty*.

1915-1920   Years of public recitations throughout the country.

1915   Publication of prose book, *The Art of the Moving Picture*. "The Chinese Nightingale" published in *Poetry* in February and awarded the magazine's $250 prize.

1

1916   Performance of children's poems at Mandel Hall, University of Chicago, with Lindsay reciting and Eleanor Dougherty dancing.

1917   *The Chinese Nightingale and Other Poems* appeared.

1920   Visit to England with his mother in the fall. Published *The Golden Whales of California.*

1921   Hike through the Rocky Mountains, Glacier Park, and Waterton Lakes Park with the English writer Stephen Graham.

1922   Death of his mother.

1923   Published *Collected Poems.*

1923-1924   Poet in residence, Gulfport Junior College, Gulfport, Mississippi.

1924   Patient at Mayo Clinic, Rochester, Minnesota; condition diagnosed as epilepsy but not made public.

1924-1925   Residence at Davenport Hotel, Spokane, Washington, writing and lecturing.

1925   Marriage to Elizabeth Conner on May 19, a Mills College graduate and the daughter of a Presbyterian clergyman. Revised edition of *Collected Poems* appeared.

1926   Daughter, Susan Doniphan Lindsay, born. *The Candle in the Cabin* published.

1927   Son, Nicholas Cave Lindsay, born.

1929   Lindsay and his family resumed residence in the parental home at Springfield. Banquet in his honor in Chicago, sponsored by *Poetry*. Published *The Litany of Washington Street*, prose essays.

1930   Awarded honorary degree, Doctor of Literature, by Hiram College.

1931   Recorded some of his poems at Columbia University in January, his only recordings. Committed suicide on December 5 by drinking Lysol.

Conrad Aiken

Vachel Lindsay

Mr. Vachel Lindsay, a few years ago, had a good deal to say of what he termed "the higher vaudeville." Mr. Lindsay's reputation, at that time, was at its brassiest and brightest. His recitations of "The Congo" and "The Chinese Nightingale" were famous, and everywhere, from Oxford even to Boston, audiences were eager to roar like lions for him. One cannot be certain which came first, theory or practice, but at all events it was early in the "Congo" and "General Booth" period that Mr. Lindsay began preaching his higher vaudeville doctrine; and it was at that time that one or two rude, perspicacious critics dared to suggest that Mr. Lindsay might be, as it were, digging his grave with a saxophone. By the "higher vaudeville" Mr. Lindsay meant that poetry ought, in his opinion, to be primarily an entertainment—and not only that, but a popular one. Poetry should be recited—the troubadour must be revived—and, above all, the audiences should participate. The theory was engaging, not to say startling; and defining it in practice with such brindled oddities as "Daniel," "King Solomon and

From *Collected Criticism* (New York: Oxford University Press, 1968), pp. 274-76. Reprinted by permission of Brandt & Brandt. Copyright © 1935, 1939, 1940, 1942, 1951, 1958 by Conrad Aiken.

3

the Queen of Sheba," and "The Potatoes' Dance," Mr. Lindsay
easily eclipsed his sedater contemporaries. This, certainly, was a
poetry which required no effort on the part of the reader; and it
was deliciously, dangerously, "original." Not the least of its virtues,
in the American view, was its richness in topical allusion (ranging
all the way from Mary Pickford to John L. Sullivan and the Anti-
Saloon League) and its patent morality—Mr. Lindsay was clearly
a sort of puritan zealot, the Bryan of poetry. In the English view,
Mr. Lindsay was seductive largely because he was so shining an
example of the barbaric yawp. His poetry, like that of Joaquin
Miller and Bret Harte, came with the proper Wild West creden-
tials. It yelled, and it wore a sombrero.

But the rude, perspicacious critics worried Mr. Lindsay. The
"high seriousness" of which they unseasonably reminded him
made him a little uneasy and furtive with his saxophone, and he
began keeping it out of sight. He not only dropped his doctrine of
the "higher vaudeville"—he even suggested that recitation, and
the writing of poetry for recitation, had not been of his own
choice, but had been forced upon him by his audiences. He added,
adroitly, that he was far more interested in drawing and hieroglyphics than in writing, and that in a great many instances the
poem was merely a descriptive title written for, and after, a drawing. The motive beneath this singular change of heart becomes
quite clear, finally, in the ambling, confidential autobiographical
preface with which Mr. Lindsay now introduces his *Collected
Poems*; it is a passionate, a pathetic desire for respectability. He
wants to be taken seriously—he wants not only audiences, but
critics too, to roar for him. At great pains, therefore, to assure us
that he is not a mere "wild man," he offers evidence that his childhood was passed in an environment not innocent of culture. Before
his fourteenth year he read Poe, and Woodberry's *Life of Poe*—
"every inch of it." He participated, as a Cupid clad in mosquito-
netting, in *Olympus*, a kind of Greek miracle-play written by his
mother—the part of Venus being taken by his Methodist Sunday-
school teacher. He was sent to a "breathlessly exclusive" drawing-
school. "Literature was taken for granted": that is, he was drilled
in reciting "choice verses" from the Bible. He read "the Brownings
and the Pre-Raphaelites." He "knew and loved in infancy the lines
of Keats—'Heard melodies are sweet.' " And the amount of time
he spent in museums lecturing on "the Ionic and Doric elements
in the evolution of the Parthenon," or drawing casts of the Elgin
marbles, is astounding. I, who have done all this, he cries, "am

assumed to hate the classics and champion their destruction. I, who have spent delightful years in the corridors of cool museums, am assumed to love noise and hate quiet." It is a cruel misconception. And the "Kallyope Yell," a case in point, seeming perhaps to prove that he likes noise, he defends on the ground that it is really intended to be *whispered*. In fact, he adds, "all my verses marked to be read aloud, should be whispered, however contradictory that may seem."

Well, unfortunately or fortunately, there is also the verse of Mr. Lindsay, which is noisy or nothing. We need not take too sagely Mr. Lindsay's petition that we judge it "for lifetime and even hereditary thoughts and memories of painting"; nor need we scrutinize it too passionately for "evidence of experience in drawing from life, drawing architecture, drawing sculpture, trying to draw the Venus de Milo, and imitating the Japanese prints and Beardsley, and trying to draw like Blake." One might as well try to tie knots in eggs. But the verse itself, if we do not ask too much of it, can be enjoyed—a little of it. "The Chinese Nightingale" and the moon poems have charm and color (color uncertainly and coarsely used), and "The Congo," "The Santa Fé Trail," and "The Fireman's Ball" have a delightful, unrestrained, vaudeville vigor and humor. The ragtime rhythms are amusing, the use of sonorous vowel sounds is broad and lavish, and in general Mr. Lindsay has gusto and what one vaguely calls "originality." But when one has said that, one has said everything. Mr. Lindsay has little mind, and little sensibility; his poetry is imageless, its ideas are childish; and as verse it is extraordinarily amateurish. One reads it, ultimately, only because Mr. Lindsay had a reputation, and because in queer corners he still has an influence. And one foresees no future for it whatever. It is the business of the poet to delight with beauty, or to amaze with understanding; and Mr. Lindsay does neither.

Harriet Monroe

Vachel Lindsay

As I write, it is ten years to a month since Mr. Yeats, at POETRY's first banquet, saluted an obscure young American and officially welcomed him into the guild of bards. Ten years to a month since this young poet of central Illinois, whose *General Booth* had appeared in POETRY more than a year earlier, responded to the elder man's compliment by reciting for the first time a new poem then unpublished, *The Congo*.

Each of these two poems afterwards entitled a book, and these two books were followed by *The Chinese Nightingale, The Golden Whales* and *Going to the Sun*—nay, even, only last summer, by *Collected Poems*. And the obscure aspirant of ten years ago has become probably the best and furthest known of all our American poets of this vocal decade. Surely it is time to pause and take account of him, not piecemeal but as a unit; to find out what he has done and whither he is going, and to question ourselves as well in regard to our attitude toward his art.

Lindsay is his mother's son, but born under a moon of magic that turned his horoscope the other way around. Somehow her

From *Poetry*, XXIV (May 1924), 90-95. Reprinted by permission of the Editor of *Poetry*. Copyright 1924 by The Modern Poetry Association.

aggressive missionary spirit, which all her life dominated the women's committees of her church and sect, was glinted with romance in this ugly duckling of a son, making him a mediaeval crusader in a world forgetful of chivalry. Of course she didn't know what to make of her slow-developing, reluctant-minded youngling. Decreeing Hiram College and a medical career to him as autocratically as a pan-cake breakfast, she was flabbergasted when she encountered a will as firm as her own and found him stubbornly preferring art.

It was a long formative period with this youth—fifteen years of dogged persistence in his own course, against bewilderment in his family and ridicule in his town, from the time he entered Hiram in 1897 until in 1912 he emerged as a poet with *General Booth.* They were years of hard precarious fare, stubborn devotion, and no doubt serious discouragement. For he did not make much headway as a student at the Art Institute of Chicago, and under Chase and Henri in New York, where for five years from 1900 he was aiming at the wrong art. Not much headway as a painter, though the educational discipline of that service and of the lecture-period that followed—years of trying to draw, of earning money as instructor-guide in museums, of plunging into Egyptian art and other oriental lore—was inestimably valuable to a crude boy out of a middle-western town; so that when the Lindsays, in a lavish moment, took their incomprehensible son abroad, they found him equipped for the trip far beyond their own provincial standards.

Then Springfield once more, and that winter of 1909-10, when the preacher-strain in him almost conquered and we find him an itinerant lecturer for the Anti-saloon League—a winter illuminated by the dim dawning of a consciousness that his own special art was poetry. At last *The Village Magazine,* rounded out to picturesque perfection by the demand it made upon all his arts—typographic, limnal and literary, and upon his purse as well. And finally his sturdy answer to the neighborhood questioning of his muse's implacable call, an answer which started him on the road, penniless and afoot, to try out his vocation in the ancient way—as a beggar dependent upon nature and simple people, and exchanging his rhymes for bread.

It was then—the autumn of 1912—that I came across his vagabond tracks in some magazine article he had written describing his adventures. And it was inevitable that the editor of a new little poet's magazine should write requesting a look at some of those rhymes it told about. Not so inevitable, however, that the response should be *General Booth*, a poem which had sung itself into his mind as he tramped along western trails. And by the time it appeared, in the New Year number of 1913, the poet—blond-haired, blue-eyed, beetle-browed; tramp, prohibitionist, campaigner for beauty—had added fuel to the fire of his poem by reading it to us with his own big voice.

From that time Lindsay's story is legible in seven or eight books of verse and prose, and especially in the *Collected Poems*. It is a consistent story; it has admirable unity. From the first this poet has been led by certain sacred and impassioned articles of faith— faith in beauty, in goodness (even human goodness, especially that of women), in the splendor of common things and common experiences; faith so sure, so living, that it fed rapturously upon the present and never sought refuge in the past. These articles of faith may sound old-fashioned or eternal, according to one's temperament; at least they have upheld the banners of all the crusades ever fought, and will march proudly on, no doubt, till the end of time.

Indeed, Lindsay is a modern knight-errant, the Don Quixote of our so-called unbelieving, unromantic age. To say this is not scorn but praise, for Don Quixote's figure looms heroically tall in perspective, and his quests, however immediately futile, become triumphant in the final account. Lindsay's whimsical imagination, even as the madder fancy of Cervantes' hero, cuts the light into seven colors like a prism, so that facts become glamorous before our eyes. Booth strides, full-haloed, into a Salvation Army heaven; fat black bucks of South State Street dance along a mystical glorified Congo; motor-cars on a Kansas road are chariots from now to forever; Bryan "sketches a silver Zion"; Johnny Appleseed is a wandering god of the soil, as mythical as Ceres; our yellow neighbor the Chinese laundryman is a son of Confucius, and his nightingale utters deathless beauty. Lindsay links up the electric sign with the stars:

> The signs in the street and the signs in the skies
> Shall make a new Zodiac, guiding the wise.

And sometimes, not always, he does this so effectively that we believe him. For his art, at its best, is adequate; Rosinante becomes Pegasus and soars beyond the moon.

It is appropriate that the American sense of humor should be, in this poet's mind, the law of perspective which ensures sanity.

Looking over a Sunday comic supplement the other day, I felt that it is in such laughter that hate dies among us. The neighborhood rages of Europe break into absurdity against it; if not the fire under the melting-pot, it is at least the crackling gas in the fuel. If Europe could only laugh as universally, as nonsensically, the heroic pose of war would become as impossible among her quarreling nations as among our forty-eight widely differing states.

Lindsay's sense of humor is true to type in its extreme variety; a faint and wistful smile, yearning for elusive and everlasting beauty, in *The Chinese Nightingale*, it becomes a sly grin in *So Much the Worse for Boston*, a tenderly sympathetic laugh in *Bryan, Bryan*, a louder laugh in *The Santa Fe Trail* or *The Kallyope Yell*, and a real guffaw in *Samson*. But the laugh, whether whispered or loud, is always genial, is never a satiric cackle. Often there is a wistful pathos in it, the trace of those tears which spring from the same bubbling fountain of human sympathy. Like the Chinese philosopher squinting at the cataract, Lindsay feels the tragedy—he is aware of the littleness of man. And to know man's littleness is to know also his greatness, for the point of the cosmic joke lies in the contrast. One finds man's greatness implied throughout the four hundred pages of Mr. Lindsay's volume, and expressed without even the reservation of a smile in such triumphant or tragic poems as *General Booth, John Brown, Eagle Forgotten*, and *Abraham Lincoln Walks at Midnight*.

If this poet was born into a rather thin and bloodless strain of puritan thought, his instinct for beauty led him early into richer regions. He has loved the mediaeval lily and the oriental lotus, even the scarlet African orchid; and has given us, if not their precise form and color, at least something of their several perfumes. Mr. Lindsay's mind, while child-like in certain aspects, is surprisingly sagacious in others. If one finds his thinking trivial at times, all of a sudden one may be astonished by such an evidence of searching critical insight as his recent article on Whitman in the *New Republic*. He is full of profound intuitions, and if he gropes among them sometimes, it is because his own awkward slow-moving self gets in his way and keeps him from turning on the light. But the light is there.

Lindsay imparts a new flare of whimsical and colorful beauty to this American scene, and presents its extraordinary variety of emotion and mood. It is a generous gift—it makes us aware of ourselves in the true tradition of authentic art the world over. And the gift is not likely to diminish seriously in value under the chemical tests of time.

Herbert S. Gorman

Vachel Lindsay: Evangelist of Poetry

It does not compel any perversion of logic to regard Vachel Lindsay as an inclusive representative of one of the three major manifestations in contemporary American poetry. Likewise he is a pivotal point and his influence will, in some measure, establish one of the potential roads in the future of our autochthonous verse. It is a peculiar fact that he is the one important figure of our day who seems to have attracted to himself no disciples, at least to the obvious extent to which Mr. Robinson, Mr. Frost and Mr. Masters have surrounded themselves with lesser atomies. His influence is of a more general sort; it is an atmosphere and not an attitude. It is this atmosphere, this subtle impregnation of the surrounding scene, that will manifest itself in the unmistakably opening roads which lead to the future American poetry. One aspect of that future is implied in noting that the roads will be plural. Our native poetry does not concentrate as poetry has done in some countries; it does not travel toward a unified expression. Indeed, the opposite is true. The variety of poets and the immensely dissimilar modes of conception are far greater today than

From *North American Review,* CCXIX (January 1924), 123-28.

they have been at any time in our history. At the same time they
are more essentially American, less dependent on the cultural
impulses of England. This, of course, is one reason for the diffuse-
ness and variability of our national inspiration today. We have
eventually discovered (long after Walt Whitman) our amazing
variety and virility. In order to intimate (generally, of course)
why Vachel Lindsay is a pivotal point in this variegated literature
—so much of it admittedly tentative—it is necessary to point out
briefly what he represents.

There are certain intellectual traits and emotional urges which
we regard as peculiarly American. It is from the reasonable juxtaposition and fine marriage of these urges that our native literature
is due to issue. For instance, there is that calm New England
reticence revealing life by side-glances, which we associate with
the name of Edwin Arlington Robinson. Another urge is the crude,
often shapeless, dynamic utterance that is best represented by the
poetry of Edgar Lee Masters. And the third manifestation, to
which I attach the name of Vachel Lindsay, is a virile evangelism,
the reforming and revivalistic spirit rarified into literature. Of
course there are other modes of literary expression, but none, I
think, so peculiarly our own as the three enumerated above. There
is the mental attitude toward life, certainly not American; and
there is the sentimental attitude, assuredly American, but (it may
be affirmed with equal assurance) now a decaying tradition, the
weapon of secondary practitioners and no longer to be discovered
in the front rank of those writers who are formulating the basic
premises for the literature of tomorrow. Assuming, therefore, that
the three urges I have noted are the most important, it is easily
perceptible how important the status of Vachel Lindsay may be
in the development of our poetry. For some reason we expect the
majority of manifestations of the evangelistic spirit to emanate
from the Middle West. It comes more naturally from Hiram College, which is Mr. Lindsay's Alma Mater, than it does from
Harvard University, for instance. It is not so much that the closely
settled East is more effete or less religious; the real reason seems
to be that the Middle West is more naïve, and naïveté is nearly
always a necessary corollary to evangelism. A man must be simple
to be convinced that he has a mission. It also requires a lack of
self consciousness. Anyone who has ever heard Vachel Lindsay
recite will bear witness to the fact that he is not self conscious.

Now this poet is a pivotal point in American poetry in so far as
he possesses the power to impress the fascination of the evangelis-

tic attitude upon younger writers. Evangelism, as I have written, is a form of spiritual activity particularly attractive to a certain type of the American mind. At its worst it results in professional reformers and Harold Bell Wrights; at its best it can climb to the heights of a Garrison, even an Abraham Lincoln. The evangelistic mind, after all, is only the intense desire to better mankind which has upset individualism and expressed itself in actual exertion. Whether or not it is wise for too many creative artists to act under this impulse is a moot question. Indeed, it is still arguable whether or not letters have anything to do with social propaganda. At the same time, it is manifest that they did have a lot to do with it during the formative period of our letters. But the doubt remains. There were many prophets, it will be remembered, and not all of them were true prophets. And evangelism often has a deplorable way of hardening into an obsession. Some of the greatest tyrants were perverted evangelists.

There would be no need to dwell upon this subject if it were not for the fact that a well defined strain of American blood responds with the utmost alacrity to the evangelistic urge. Messianic delusions are a yearly crop in this country, and there are enough self appointed angels to reach from here to Mars. Vachel Lindsay has not progressed to that exalted state where he regards himself as a Messiah, and it is perfectly evident that he will never reach that perilous predicament because he possesses altogether too much common sense. Allied with his common sense is an uncommon sense of humour, a trait that is generally defunct in the typical reformer. But in spite of these agreeable possessions Lindsay very clearly gives evidence of the evangelistic streak. There is hardly a poem which he has written that is not marked with that impulse somewhere. His *Collected Poems*, for instance, is more than a mere book; it is a weapon, a whole armoury of weapons, with which he has steadfastly fought on the side of the angels against the Powers of Darkness. He slashes out against greed, political chicanery, militarism, alcohol, war, capitalistic oppression, and all preservations of unequalities. He is frankly religious time and again with a vehemence that is almost stentorian. An essentially modern knight, he whacks away at vice with a resounding rhythm that sounds like a stuffed club. Yet there is a horseshoe in that club. He is as vigorous in his love of humanity as Walt Whitman.

Many of his poems are hymns of praise, visions of a golden future (a Utopia of gentleness, justice, charity and skyscrapers) when the lion will lie down in cosy amity with the lamb; above all, the high song of brotherliness and love. He has written a *Litany of the Heroes* in which he roundly praises all those great minds which have aided Mankind in its long and difficult progress up the bloody slopes of Time. Because Vachel Lindsay is adapted to this sort of expression, because it is born and bred in his bones and is woven like a golden thread through his mind, he is thoroughly successful in handling subjects that would be but jaded repetitions of old truisms from the pen of a lesser writer. Everything he writes is the direct result of a strong and authentic emotion. To this bold evangelism he has brought a sweet reasonableness, a rare and delightful sense of humour, and a metrical emphasis that has been, to say the least, unusual.

A word should be written about this metrical emphasis. Lindsay himself has pointed out that his readers have given his so-called "jazz" poems an importance far out of their due, that they form but a small proportion of his work, and that he desires in no wise to be regarded as an exponent of what has been termed "the higher vaudeville". Such poems as *The Kallyope Yell, The Congo* and several others occupy but a few pages in the *Collected Poems.* They are delicious, particularly so when Lindsay recites them in a sonorous voice, but they can hardly be regarded as the essential Lindsay. Like all revivalists, he has his loud moments; like most sincere revivalists he has those other more important moments when the voice is softer and the passion more intense. The real Lindsay is implicit in such poems as *The Chinese Nightingale, I Know All This When Gypsy Fiddles Cry, In Praise of Johnny Appleseed, Abraham Lincoln Walks at Midnight,* the delicately conceived series of moon poems, *When the Mississippi Flowed in Indiana,* and *The Eagle That is Forgotten.* He is to be found in such a personal revelation (although practically every poem which Lindsay has written is, in some measure, a personal revelation) as *My Fathers Came from Kentucky,* which is well worth setting down as a self-portrait:

> I was born in Illinois,—
> Have lived there many days.
> And I have Northern words,
> And thoughts,
> And ways.
>
> But my great-grandfathers came
> To the west with Daniel Boone,

And taught his babes to read,
And heard the redbird's tune;

And heard the turkey's call,
And stilled the panther's cry,
And rolled on the blue-grass hills,
And looked God in the eye.

And feud and Hell were theirs;
Love, like the moon's desire,
Love like a burning-mine,
Love like rifle-fire.

I tell tales out of school
Till these Yankees hate my style.
Why should the young cad cry,
Shout with joy for a mile?

Why do I faint with love
Till the prairies dip and reel?
My heart is a kicking horse
Shod with Kentucky steel.

No drop of my blood from north
Of Mason and Dixon's line.
And this racer in my breast
Tears my ribs for a sign.

But I ran in Kentucky hills
Last week. They were hearth and home. . . .
And the church at Grassy Springs,
Under the redbird's wings
Was peace and honeycomb.

In such a poem as this we find the vehemence (it takes a fine writer to flare naturally into such phrases as "love like rifle-fire" and "my heart is a kicking horse shod with Kentucky steel"), the intense ardour and passion of the real Lindsay. He does not require "boomlays" and such exclamations to drive the magic home.

I have said that naïveté is a necessary corollary of evangelism, and considered from certain aspects Vachel Lindsay is the most naïve poet that we have. His heart is always exposed. His passions are unveiled. He is unique in his spontaneous giving of himself to the casual reader. There is a clean, childlike quality about him, and it comes most naturally when we observe him fashioning dance poems for children or moon poems which are first of all children's rhymes and only secondarily meant for adults. Like Rupert Brooke, although in a far different way, he is a great lover. Brooke's passions were mainly sensory. He loved bright colours, things he could see like plates and grasses and holes in the ground, things he could taste and smell and touch. Lindsay's love is more an adoration of the spirit, an intimate sensing of natures and personalities. This emotion floods the autobiographical introduction to his *Collected Poems*, and there, too, we find many hints concerning the genesis of his abilities and achievements. He was an art student for many years (no one knows Lindsay who has not seen his amusing drawings) and many of his shorter poems were written for pictures. He possesses unusual ideas about the alphabet, and he maintains that he is working toward an American hieroglyphic. His enthusiasm for these things is the enthusiasm of a boy; loud, infectious.

It is true that he has lapses as a poet. Sometimes his thought outruns his content and the result is a ragged poem. Many of his pieces are light as thistledown, unimportant bits flung off at random, and the fact that he includes them in his printed volumes has caused astonishment in some quarters. But Lindsay must be taken as he gives himself, whole-heartedly. It is part of his naïveté that he is not selective. He just pours out everything until the whole man is before the reader. No other American poet has so given himself to his readers. No other has been so confirmed in his conviction of a mission. If he does influence young men into an evangelistical type of literature, they cannot go far wrong if they go no farther than he does and with as exalted a spirit. But young men generally take a hint and then make their own road thereafter, and a good evangelist often has poor disciples who pervert their mission. After all, there can be but one touchstone for poetry, and that is art. If it is that, it may be anything else it pleases. Lindsay, when he is at his best, is art. The fact that it is often achieved unconsciously no whit lessens its value.

Albert Edmund Trombly

Vachel Lindsay's Prose

Of Mr. Lindsay's prose books, the most enduring will doubtless be the *Handy Guide* and the *Adventures*. *The Art of the Moving Picture* and the *Golden Book of Springfield* add nothing to the man's merit as a prose writer, though they make clearer his doctrine of America redeemed through beauty; a doctrine, the essential truth of which is inevitable, however long we may remain deaf to it and however many more enthusiasts must rise up to proclaim it. But since I have chosen to discuss only the best of Mr. Lindsay's prose writings, I must confine myself to the two earlier books. Like the best of his poems, they are unique. They are better written, sustained at a higher level, than any of his books of poems, and a generation hence they will be as fresh and readable as they are today. In originality, in native flavor and charm, they must rank with the best prose books which Americans have written.

A Handy Guide For Beggars is the record of the tramping journeys undertaken from New York in the spring of 1906 and the spring of 1908; and although it was not published (1916)

From *Southwest Review,* XIII (July 1928), 459-68. Reprinted by permission of Southern Methodist University.

until after the *Adventures* (1914), it records earlier experiences. Thus the sequence followed in my discussion is that of the events recorded rather than of the publication of the books.

The first expedition led the poet through Georgia, North Carolina, Tennessee, and Kentucky; while the second took him through New Jersey and Pennsylvania westward to Hiram, Ohio.

"There are one hundred new poets in the villages of the land. This *Handy Guide* is dedicated first of all to *them*." It is dedicated also to all the outcasts and daydreamers who flaunt their pride and rebellion like banners. Yet I defy any sympathetic reader to believe that the book is not dedicated to him personally. It takes us all out of home, shop, office, class-room, pulpit, and fields, and allures us down the road where we saunter along at one with our guide, who, in turn, is at one with his beloved St. Francis "in the presence of the beneficent sun". The book is one of spiritual regeneration through contact with sincere and primal things. It is a book for business men, politicians, preachers in comfortable pulpits, professors of literature, ladies, "new" poets, and no end of others. We all need a bath in the Falls of Tallulah; all need to ride in a caboose beside the Man with Apple-green Eyes; all need a night's lodging in The House of the Loom. Then will business men have learned how to make less money, which is what they need to know; the politicians will serve their constituents; the comfortable preachers will exhort the soil with a plow six days a week instead of unregenerate mortals, with guarded words, one day a week; the professors will talk about men and life instead of dusty books and dates of publications; the ladies will take on the ways of women; the "new" poets will whistle behind a yoke of oxen; and the "no end of others" will contribute what they can to the holy order of the brotherhood of man.

What I mean is that no one can read this book without questioning much of the sophistication with which we hedge ourselves in so smugly and uncomfortably. We share in Mr. Lindsay's reverence for the simple and profound virtues, the patriarchal living which he found among the good folk who gave him food and shelter; and if we have the goodness of heart and sanity, we shall wish that we too had the courage to turn beggar.

The book is not a sermon, it is a holiday. It is a call away from the iron wheels of commercial and industrial centers to the sauntering gait of the open road and the kindly hearts of an elemental people. Mr. Lindsay has turned tramp because his soul had become clogged with factory smoke and needs an airing. It could not function properly, could not serve mankind efficiently until it was cleansed and made whole again. And who, if he have the courage and vision, would not follow at times the path which "wanders back through history till it encounters Tramp Columbus, Tramp Dante, Tramp St. Francis, Tramp Buddha, and the rest of our masters"?

But remember that this tramping is not a vocation; merely an experiment. And when this experiment has been tried, life will still hold out a variety of others. When Thoreau had lived his two years or so at Walden Pond, he knew what such an experiment had proved and could prove; but he wanted to try others. He stood ready to return to that mode of living if he saw fit, but he was under no obligations to it. So too with Mr. Lindsay.

> I took to the road once, long ago, because people said if I staid rhymer and artist I would be a beggar and die in the poor-house. My most intimate friends prophesied it incessantly for years, after nourishing themselves on business men's clubs and office-supply advertisements. Therefore, in no sentimental mood, but actually to try out this beggary, and deliberately calling myself "a beggar to the end of my days", I took to the road, and tried, as it were, the "poor-house", at its worst, that I might get used to it.
>
> People are far too sentimental about my begging days and talk as though they were over. I stand ready to beg tomorrow to the end of the chapter, rather than write a line I do not want to write, recite for a routine audience, or go through any parrot or ape performances, even if I am parroting and aping what I myself happened to be twenty-four hours ago.

No one can forget the people he has met along the road of the *Handy Guide*: Napoleon the Third (a traveling salesman who wore moustaches like the Emperor's), the Gnome, the Old Lady at the Top of the Hill, Lady Iron-Heels, Gretchen-Cecilia, and a host of others. No attempt has been made to create them; they are part of the living text, and he who has read the book has met and knows them.

The humor of the book is as spontaneous and artless as the characters. Nothing could be more delightful than the chapter called *Man In The City Of Collars*; and like the collar-salesman, the reader succumbs to the author's Ancient-Mariner eye and mesmeric rhymes.

Much of Mr. Lindsay's humor lies in his seemingly artless satire. On one occasion he spends a night at a mission in the "richest village in New Jersey". A series of incidents, during which the poet is treated as if he were an escaped convict, culminates in an argument with the "attendant" as to whether the poet must wear to bed pajamas which have been worn by most of the tramps in America with never a wash-day interim. Poetlike, he gets the worst of the argument:

> "Blessed are the meek, for they shall inherit the earth," I said to myself, and put on the pajamas. . .
> The lights went out. I kicked off the pajamas and slept. I awoke at midnight and reflected on all these matters. I quoted another scripture to myself: "I was naked, and ye clothed me."

However, his satire often shows another sting; and we might recommend to those who see in him a sort of rhyme-chanting Y. M. C. A. secretary *The Sermon On The Mount* of *Handy Guide* fame. We are still in the mission which clothed him when he was naked, and the clergyman appears, to help the mission in its "problem".

> An unmitigated clergyman rose to read a text. I presume this clergyman imagined Christ wore a white tie and was on a salary promptly paid by some of our oldest families. But I share with the followers of St. Francis the vision of Christ as a man of the open road, improvident as the sparrow. I share with the followers of Tolstoi the opinion that when Christ proclaimed those uncomfortable social doctrines, he meant what he said.

The mention of St. Francis is not accidental. He is the patron saint of the *Handy Guide*; and he who knows the *Laudi* will find more than one echo of the praises of the "beneficent sun" in Mr. Lindsay's writings. In the spiritual strength which renounces the comfortable paths of the world for the humble one which leads to the brotherhood of men, is there not a certain kinship between the lovable saint and the advocate of the gospel of beauty?

There is an inevitable resemblance between the *Adventures While Preaching The Gospel Of Beauty* (1914) and the *Handy Guide For Beggars*. Both are records of tramping expeditions; both are planned in about the same way; and the *Adventures* seem like a continuation of the *Handy Guide*. The former is, for the most part, a series of letters written home "from the front"; the latter is more like the amplification of diary notes. Then, too, there is more continuity in the narrative of the *Adventures*. Once more there is need for spiritual recuperation, since the period (1908-12) in which the crusader has been trying to convert his hometown to the new localism has been strenuous and exhausting. Besides, the road holds out another promise. Mr. Lindsay's hope for democracy in America is rooted in his faith in America made beautiful. For the time being, at least, the machine-made and machine-maintained cities are sterile ground. No seed of beauty can take root there. But in the hamlets, the agricultural villages, where are found the patriarchal families, the "blacksmith aristocracy", there will be found also the soil which awaits the seed. So with a packful of rhymes, and posters that expound the gospel of beauty, this Johnny Appleseed tramps across the farmlands of Missouri and Kansas. Again he exchanges his rhymes for bread (or whatever substitute is offered him) and nails his posters to fences where the farmers will be sure to see them. Even the irate farmer who discharges the poet because the latter's physique gives out in the midst of harvesting, cannot escape the rhymes which the poet hands him as he takes his leave.

As early as the *Village Magazine* (1910) the gospel of beauty had been pretty clearly defined. It was the new localism seeking to make of the home-town a center of democratic art. The crusader now proposed to sow this doctrine broadcast through the Middle West.

The talented children of every village were to be given an art education, one that would voice the democratic aspirations of the nation. Then as painters, sculptors, architects, dancers, craftsmen, and poets, they would return to their native villages, where each would expound and develop his particular art. And no less earnest than their faith in art was to be their faith in the righteousness of God. It was fortunate and inevitable that the new gospel should have the religious tenet; fortunate, because it would not antagonize the simple folk for whom it was destined; inevitable because it is a necessary part of Mr. Lindsay's creed. There are times when the poet's religious enthusiasm has made for preaching instead of art; but at others, as in the Booth poem, he has fused successfully the poetic and the religious. And because the man's religious attitude is genuine, we cannot believe that the religious tenet in the gospel of beauty is merely a deft attempt at sugar-coating.

The posters which the Adventurer carried were reproductions of drawings for *The Village Improvement Parade,* and conspicuous among the *Rhymes To Be Traded For Bread* were *The Proud*

Farmer, The Illinois Village, and *The Building Of Springfield.*
These three poems gave the "best brief expression of my gospel".

The sceptic will shrug his shoulders, laugh, and doubt (far more,
perhaps, than did the simple folk to whom the gospel was ex-
pounded); he may even go so far as to doubt the Adventurer's
sanity or offer him a job with the railroad section-gang. But why
should we agree with the sceptic? Beauty strikes us in too subtle
ways for that; and the seeds of the gospel of beauty which the
Adventurer has sown will as surely sprout, grow, and bear fruit as
did the appleseeds of Johnny Appleseed generations ago.

Now it so happened that as the Adventurer fared westward a
new and vast horizon loomed up before him—harvest-time in
Kansas; and the book which begins as an exposition of the gospel
of beauty takes a sudden turn and becomes the passionate song of
the great wheat harvest. It is undoubtedly the finest piece of writing which has been inspired by this particular phase of our
national life; and those who do not share the feeling that it is the
epic of the western harvest, may grant that Mr. Lindsay has
shown our future poets the road and the method.

When the Adventurer comes upon the harvest, the book takes
a sudden turn. What happens is this. The apostle who has set out
to preach the gospel of beauty, finds a larger and more eloquent
one than he had dreamed, identifies himself with it, and returns
with a much larger pack than that with which he had started. His
faith in the agricultural village, in the rural population, in true
democracy for America, has increased a hundred-fold. The never-
ending expanse of the Kansas wheat fields has entered into his
soul. America will listen to the gospel of beauty and she will be
redeemed.

Without being metaphysical, Mr. Lindsay is profoundly interested in men. He observes them shrewdly, and understands them
with rare insight and sympathy. In his suggestions for social reform he is always sound, and doubtless because he prefers to give
rather than to extort. An old couple who have the care of a
stationary engine are representative of present-day humanity and
prove to him once more that man has surrendered his individuality
to a machine. And let us not forget that Mr. Lindsay was one of
the first to point this out as a cause of social unrest. "Poor things!
Just like all the citizens of the twentieth century, petting and
grooming machinery three times as smart as they are themselves.
Such people should have engines to take care of them, instead of
taking care of engines." And in stating his economic position, he

sets forth truths not acceptable to certain classes, but bound to prevail in this country sooner or later:

> I have thought of a new way of stating my economic position. I belong to one of the leisure classes, that of the rhymers. In order to belong to any leisure class, one must be a thief or a beggar. On the whole I prefer to be a beggar, and, before each meal, receive from toiling man new permission to extend my holiday. The great business of that world that looms above the workshop and the furrow is to take things from people by some sort of taxation or tariff or special privilege. But I want to exercise my covetousness only in a retail way, open and aboveboard, and when I take bread from a man's table I want to ask him for that particular piece of bread as politely as I can.

As of the *Handy Guide*, St. Francis is the patron saint of the *Adventures*. He is invoked repeatedly; and his benignity and compassion inform the book throughout. Here, for example, is the very quintessence of Franciscan charity. The Adventurer is speaking of the two old keepers of the engine whom we met above:

> But seldom are keepers of engine-stables as unfortunate as these. The best they can get from the world is cruel laughter. Yet this woman, crippled in brain, her soul only half alive, this dull man, crippled in body, had God's gift of the liberal heart. If they are supremely absurd, so are all of us. We must include ourselves in the farce. These two, tottering through the dimness and vexation of our queer world, were willing the stranger should lean upon them. I say they had the good gift of the liberal heart. One thing was theirs to divide. That was a roof. They gave me my third and they helped me to hide from the rain. In the name of St. Francis I laid me down. May that saint of all saints be with them, and with all the gentle and innocent and weary and broken.

The incidents are always picturesque, often humorous, always fascinating. What more flattering to a knight of the road than to look so much like a Gypsy as to be mistaken for one by the Gypsies themselves! The reader is not likely to forget the stop at the section-gang's shanty, and the Adventurer's request to the men who are throwing through the open door perfectly good sandwiches and pieces of pie, that they wait until he get out there to catch them; nor the occasion on which the schoolmaster "gets the poet's goat" for doubting his authorship of the poems he has been reading; nor the harvest hand who puts by his pornographic rhymes in favor of the chorus from *Atalanta in Calydon.*

Then, too, the reader or hearer of Mr. Lindsay's poems will find in the Adventures the sources, so to speak, of *The Santa Fé Trail.* The old negro who explains that a certain bird is the Rachel Jane; the automobiles with their horns and pennants; the fast trains; the hand cars; the good folk who stare at the crank drawings; the strawberries by the roadside; the grasshoppers that eat holes in a man's shirt—all are there. And the account of *The Broncho That Would Not Be Broken Of Dancing* is not only masterly prose, but a finer piece of verbal expression than the poem—good though it be—on the same subject.

Carl Van Doren

Salvation With Jazz

Church and state in the United States are allied at least to this degree: reforms and revivals take lessons from each other. The rhythm of each is the rhythm of crusade. When souls or cities are to be saved, the tambourine must be shaken, the trombone must disturb the sky. The roots of the American revival go back to Jonathan Edwards, that Peter the Hermit of New England, who found his people sunk in the dullness of prose and sought to lift them up and draw them after him in a march upon the City of God which he believed might be discovered, or established, on their own soil. The roots of American reform go back to the poets and orators of the Revolution, who found their people accepting too tamely the smug rule of Great Britain, and taught them to hope and work for a republic of mankind which was to replace their ancient form of government when they should have put forth efforts heroic enough to earn a republic. The Great Awakening and the Glorious Revolution thus early set the pace and called the dance which have continued ever since. Even when, as in many

From *Many Minds* (New York: Alfred A. Knopf, 1924), pp. 151-66. Reprinted by permission of Margaret Bevans, executrix of the author's estate. Copyright by the estate of Carl Van Doren.

of its aspects, American life has become doggedly or venomously reactionary, the rhythm of crusade has kept on throbbing in the popular imagination. Theodore Roosevelt is but the archetype of countless strenuous Americans who, fired by a vision of civil excellence, start the bagpipes skirling and raise a rhythmic din among their warriors as they advance toward some high political goal. Billy Sunday is but the archetype of countless strenuous natives who, inflamed with a passion for the good old cause, hang bells upon their caps, set the tom-tom going, and sweep forward, or backward, to the pulse of jazz, to the roar of camp-followers drunk with the pious opportunity.

2

Vachel Lindsay emerged from a plane of culture on which such enthusiasms flourish. He is, among recent American poets, the most impetuous enthusiast. Only he, among those recent American poets who are also important, has a record, which he avows, of membership in a more or less militant denomination, of admiration for foreign missionaries, of activities in the Young Men's Christian Association, of blows struck in behalf of the Anti-Saloon League. Other bards may see in prohibition a set of statutes against cakes and ale or an increase of tyranny deftly managed by clever lobbyists in the interests of a comfortable minority with stocks in its cellars; to Mr. Lindsay the prohibition movement is, or was, a gallant revolution against the sour and savage King Alcohol who has too long ruled the race. Others may see in Y.M.C.A. secretaries the least imaginative of those persons who believe that a Christian should be all things to all men, and may see in foreign missionaries the least imaginative of those persons who believe that God should be one thing to all men; to Mr. Lindsay such secretaries and missionaries are, or were, knights and paladins whose quarrels are just, whose conquests are beneficent, because they uphold and extend the healing hands of Christ. Others may see in the Campbellites an undistinguished, though aggressive, village sect with apostolic prejudices; to Mr. Lindsay the Disciples are the faithful legionaries of Alexander Campbell, the pioneer who proclaimed a millennium in the Western wilderness and set the feet of his companions and inheritors on the path which leads to a New Jerusalem.

Most of the poems in which Mr. Lindsay utters or hints at these opinions are early, and most of them are, as poems, trash. They are not, however, the whole story. They are merely items in his attempt to give his work a basis in the moods and in the

rhythms of his native section. As a student of art in Chicago and
in New York he was not entirely at home; he could not find a
natural idiom to match his impulses. That idiom he eventually
found in a language which expresses the mood of the local patriot
in the rhythm of national vaudeville. He devised the terms "the
new localism" and "the higher vaudeville" to give the authority
of doctrine to his practice. Localism, of course, had long been one
of the most potent forces in the country, particularly in Mr.
Lindsay's Middle West. Town had striven with town to see which
could sing its own praises loudest and so further its own aspirations by bringing in new inhabitants and larger business. The
strife had encouraged all the natural tendencies toward optimism
and complacency, and had developed the windy lingo of the
booster until it had become perhaps the most customary oratory of
the region. Here was something, Mr. Lindsay felt, to be translated
into the worthier idiom of poetry. But he was a booster of a novel
disposition. He wanted to see brought to his town of Springfield
not more business but more beauty; not more inhabitants but
more elevation of life.

This is what Mr. Lindsay himself undertook to do. He wandered
in the South and East and got material for *A Handy Guide for
Beggars*, full of counsel for such as find themselves choked by
houses and bored by books, and so take to the open road of the
poet and the vagabond. He wandered from Illinois to New Mexico
and got material for *Adventures While Preaching the Gospel of
Beauty*, that quaint, racy, joyful narrative of his experiences while
he was about his singular evangelism. On both journeys he carried
with him his *Rhymes to Be Traded for Bread*, got food and shelter
by them, and scattered the seed of beauty on every kind of soil he
met. The good he did to others it would be hard to estimate, but
the good done to him by his adventures is unmistakable. He came
back to Springfield fully developed as a poet. Henceforth he was
to be contented to live in that inland capital. He would voice its
aspirations, he would interpret its folk-ways, he would use its
dialect, he would snare its rhythms, he would write words for the
tunes which rang through its sleepy head.

3

His creed was less original than his performance. There had
been Americans before him who had in mind to make Boston as
memorable as Athens, New York as memorable as Paris; and other
Americans who vowed to make Indianapolis as memorable as Boston, or San Francisco as memorable as New York. A European,

standing beside a river, calls it liquid history; an American, beside
a river in his own land, sees prophecy in it, and thinks what
memories are being cast upon its waters by the great deeds being
done along its banks. All that was new in Mr. Lindsay's passion
was its special object and method. He was the first to boost for
beauty in the common American language. In his earliest notable
poem, *General William Booth Enters Into Heaven*, he took the
theme of a revival sermon and the rhythm of a revival hymn and
achieved the fruitful marriage of salvation with jazz. So much is
national, but Mr. Lindsay gives his poem a touch of local color
such as any medieval painter might have given it.

> "Jesus come out from the court-house door,
> Stretched his hands above the passing poor.
> Booth saw not, but led his queer ones there,
> Round and round the mighty court-house square."

The scene of the triumphant entry is Springfield, or some town
like it; Mr. Lindsay had brought the drama of salvation home to
his own neighbors.

After piety, patriotism. If Mr. Lindsay had seen poetic possibilities in the Salvation Army, so did he see them in the spectacle
of countless motors streaming across the continent in a grandiose
pageant. As a tramping evangelist in Kansas he had at first resented the proud speed of the automobiles dashing past him, but
in time he lost his resentment in his fascination.

> "I would not walk all alone till I die
> Without some life-drunk horns going by."

Do the roaring engines and the raw horns disturb the peace of
dreams? So does the march of life always disturb them. But
dreams, after all, come back when the thunder of the proces-
sion dies. Meanwhile there is magnificence in the rush of so many
motors, each one bearing a pennant with the name of the city
from which it hails. In *The Santa Fe Trail: A Humoresque* Mr.
Lindsay reels off the names of the cities in the manner of a train-
caller in a railway station—reels them off till he is drunk with the
motley syllables and in his exaltation sees the United States go by.
Here he is even more native than in his poem on Booth, for
Booth was an Englishman who arrived in a reasonably international paradise; but the flood of automobiles pouring across Kansas, perceived by a poet crusading for the new localism, and
chanted in a manner based upon a train-caller's drone—this is
home-grown, home-spun, home-measured, home-made.

Mr. Lindsay sought, however, to go still deeper into his soil.
Springfield has Negroes among its citizens and has had race riots.
To the superficial eye these particular Americans seem to give
themselves to loose habits, hilarious amusements, fantastic religions. In the literary tradition they have regularly been regarded
as mere comic figures or as pathetic victims of oppression. The
higher vaudeville sees other aspects:

> "Then I had religion, then I had a vision.
> I could not turn from their revel in derision.
> Then I saw the Congo, creeping through the black,
> Cutting through the forest with a golden track."

These particular Americans are also Africans. The jungle is in
their blood: loud colors, powerful odors, witchcraft, malign deities.
Mr. Lindsay, observing

> "Fat black bucks in a wine-barrel room. . . .
> Beat an empty barrel with the handle of a broom,"

hears behind them

> "the boom of the blood-lust song
> And a thigh-bone beating on a tin-pan gong."

Observing crap-shooters and cake-walkers at their irrepressible
play, he sees a Negro fairy-land with gaudy revelers laughing at
the witch-doctors who try to cow them with talk of Mumbo-
Jumbo:

> "Just then from the doorway, as fat as shotes,
> Came the cake-walk princes in their long red coats,
> Canes with a brilliant lacquer shine,
> And tall silk hats that were red as wine.
> And they pranced with their butterfly partners there,
> Coal-black maidens with pearls in their hair,
> Knee-skirts trimmed with the jessamine sweet,
> And bells on their ankles and little black feet.
> And the couples railed at the chant and the frown
> Of the witch-men lean, and laughed them down."

Observing that

> "A good old negro in the slums of the town
> Preached at a sister for her velvet gown,
> Howled at a brother for his low-down ways,
> His prowling, guzzling, sneak-thief days,
> Beat on the Bible till he wore it out
> Starting the jubilee revival shout,"

the poet sees behind this familiar sight a great day along the Congo when

> "the grey sky opened like a new-rent veil
> And showed the Apostles with their coats of mail.
> In bright white steel they were seated round
> And their fire-eyes watched where the Congo wound.
> And the twelve Apostles, from their thrones on high
> Thrilled all the forest with their heavenly cry:
> "Mumbo-Jumbo will die in the jungle;
> Never again will he hoodoo you."

The anthropology of *The Congo* is hardly to be trusted. Whatever cults may have existed among the ancestors of the Afro-Americans, they themselves are most of them Baptists or Methodists, under-educated and under-privileged. Mr. Lindsay's poem is significant less as a "Study of the Negro Race" than as an example of a new poetical use to which a certain native material was ready to be put. Here more completely than anywhere else in his work he makes drama out of his reading of life. Is the plight of mankind lamentable in the jungle, among the slums, on the lone prairie? It need not be, as Mr. Lindsay sees it. Somewhere there are crusaders to bring salvation, shouting, singing, beating upon optimistic drums.

4

If Mr. Lindsay's poetry is more original than his philosophy, so is it more valuable. Like all crusaders, he has difficulty in looking ahead to the end of the bright path he follows with such rapture. *The Golden Book of Springfield*, in which he sets forth his notion of what his native town may have become by 2018, is a Utopia of Katzenjammer. History serves him better than prophecy, as when he celebrates the fame of that John Chapman who as Johnny Appleseed is remembered for his gift of orchards to the Middle West. Indeed, Mr. Lindsay is at his best when he is engaged in promoting to poetry some figure or group of figures heretofore neglected by the poets: the Salvation Army, the motorists of the Sante Fe trail, the Springfield blacks, Alexander Campbell, John Chapman, John L. Sullivan, John P. Altgeld, the Bryan of 1896.

On these occasions the poet is not content to write history merely; he makes myths. His Alexander Campbell still rides his circuit, announcing the millennium and snatching back renegade souls to the faith; his John Chapman still roams the great valley, a backwoods St. Francis, with the seeds of civilization in his wallet.

During the war, in *Abraham Lincoln Walks at Midnight*, Mr.
Lindsay thus poetically brought to life the greatest of all Springfield's citizens, to move restlessly through the streets.

"Yea, when the sick world cries, how can he sleep?"

Poetry, in a conception like this, joins hands with religion, keeping
the heroes and the saints and the gods alive because those who
depend upon them will not believe that they have died. In a
fashion like this patriotism grows up, knitting many hearts together by giving them common memories and common hopes.

And yet Vachel Lindsay is not the personage he was when he
published *The Congo* in the same year with *Spoon River Anthology*. Both he and Edgar Lee Masters were deliberately going back
to Greek models, the one to the chanted lyric, the other to the
ironical epigram. Irony, however, won the day, helped by the presence in the times of a tumult through which nothing less cutting
than the voice of irony could reach; and in the eight years since
the appearance of the two books the tendency of American literature has been steadily toward irony, satire, criticism. To the drive
for the new localism there has succeeded a revolt from the village,
turning to ridicule the eloquence of the local patriot and laughing
at the manners of the small community. To the confidence that
much might be made for literature out of the noisier, rougher elements of the national life by the process of lifting them to richer,
surer rhythms and giving them a sounder language, has succeeded
the feeling, best voiced by H. L. Mencken, that such elements are
menace, nuisance, or nonsense, and that the cause of the higher
vaudeville, to be based upon them, is not worth fighting for. Some
sense of this shift in the current literary mood must have been
responsible, at least in part, for the loss by Mr. Lindsay of the full
vigor with which he sang in those first hopeful days; for his inclination to turn away from creation to criticism and scholarship,
from poetry to design.

5

The crusader cannot be a connoisseur. He must meet the masses
of men something like halfway. Nor can it be merely in the matter
of language that he meets them. He must share as well a fair
number of their enthusiasms and antipathies. He must have gusto,
temper, rhetoric; must apply them to topics which are not too
much refined by nice distinctions. These qualities Mr. Lindsay
has, and he lets them range over a wide area of life, delighting in

more things than his reason could defend. He rejoices, too, in more things than his imagination can assimilate. For Mr. Lindsay's poetical range is not very great. His eye is bigger than his appetite. That eye embraces the Anti-Saloon League and the sons of Roosevelt and Comrade Kerensky and dozens of such morsels; he gulps them down, but no digestion follows. He is a reformer, an evangelist. He lifts his standard for all who will gather round it; he spreads his arms to all who will come to them. His business is not, as that of a different poet might be, to find only the purest gold or the clearest gems. It is rather to spade up new sod and see what unexpected flowers will spring from it; to peer into dusky corners and see that nothing precious has been hidden there; to explore the outer boundaries of the regions of poetry and see if they cannot be extended to include virgin territories hitherto unoccupied. No wonder he has made as many poetic failures as any poet of his rank.

But besides his failures, there are his successes. To appreciate them it is necessary to have heard him read his own verse. His reading is almost singing; it is certainly acting. The rhythms of the camp-meeting, of the cake-walk, of the stump-speech, of the chantey, of the soldiers' march, of patriotic songs, of childish games, throb through him and are from him communicated to the most difficult audience. His singsong is as contagious as that of any revivalist who ever exhorted; his oratory rings. The pulse of human life has beat upon him till he has left its rhythm and meter; simplifying them by his art, he turns and plays with them upon his hearers till they, too, throb in excited unison. Noise by itself, when orderly, has some poetical elements; rhythm, without tune or words, may be thrilling. The potency of Mr. Lindsay's verse, however, shows how far he goes beyond mere noise and rhythm. He has pungent phrases, clinging cadences, dramatic energy, comic thrust, lyric seriousness, tragic intensity. Though he may sprawl and slip and though a large portion of his work is simply sound without importance, he is at bottom both a person and a poet. He is, after all, like no one else. Something in him which was better than his conscious aims has taught him, however much he might borrow from the circuit-rider, the crusader, the booster, that true eloquence comes from the individual, not from the mass; that true poetry is actually lived, not merely shared or argued.

Henry Seidel Canby

Vachel Lindsay

Vachel Lindsay already takes his place in literary history. He was a bard, if any modern deserved that title. Rapt, enthusiastic, fixed in his loyalties and his inspirations, he was at the opposite spiritual edge from the intellectualism and verbal refinements of the modernists in poetry. Poetry for him was still a chant, and his sonorous, slightly nasal chanting, with upraised face and dropped eyelids, like a blind Illinois Homer, still lingers in our memories. His rhythms sought the rhythms of native speech, but unlike the cool and humorous colloquialisms of Robert Frost, it was an excited speech, like the shouts at camp meetings, or the boasts and boostings of oxmen and boatmen. Listening to him one was carried backward, not forward, back of the American folk history now being so extensively written, back of Walt Whitman, who knew what Lindsay knew, had heard what he had heard, but made over the American saga to fit Emerson's philosophy, back into an authentic minstrelsy springing from a culture not rich but deep, because in it the primitive racial instincts had been rearoused by pioneering

From *Saturday Review of Literature,* VIII (January 9, 1932), 437. Reprinted by permission of *Saturday Review.*

—the culture of the Mississippi valley, that same soil from which grew Huckleberry Finn.

And yet it would be much too simple to call Vachel Lindsay the last and best of American ballad makers. He had, in one sense, no predecessors, for the poetry of the negro, the revivalist, the frontiersman, though spiritually akin to his work, was seldom written down, seldom even formulated, and when it did struggle into print, took the conventional literary forms of its period. Only in the negro spirituals and in a very few ballads did it ever get that finality of utterance (however primitive) which makes literature. Lindsay, for all his closeness to the traditions of the common people, was not a true contemporary of the saga periods of Johnny Appleseed or of Lincoln which inspired him. He belongs historically with the recreators of American history who in the twentieth century have recovered or rewritten the eighteenth and nineteenth centuries when the continent was won. And just as the skillful historian of our time has approached the saga of Oklahoma or the Sante Fé trail with as much care for its imaginative significance as for the facts, so Lindsay tapped the reservoirs of folk poetry with a modern sense of the value of the primitive and a full realization that both saga and ballad were art. This was not the cause of his success, which was due rather to the beating of his heart in the corn-belt rhythm, but without this modern consciousness he would have been either the Eddie Guest of the ballads or a mere exploiter of folk lore.

He was neither, but, in his limited field, a powerful poet. He was perhaps the only man in those corny regions still a frontiersman in spirit and yet a self-conscious historian in verse. His genius was like one of those rich pockets of ore that are deposited where one stratum ends at the beginning of a different country rock.

And this was his personal tragedy. His vein was rich, but narrow. It was hard to keep to it without divergence, on the one side into banality, on the other into extravagance. When he was not writing "General William Booth Enters Heaven," or "The Congo," or "The Chinese Nightingale," he was trying to make psalms about a modern mid-Western capital, or poetry of people and experiences which were not only simple but flat. The sense of futility, due to the limitations wherein his genius flowered, showed itself in constant attempts to escape. Once he besought his friends in editorial offices to boom his reputation as an art critic, for that was going to be his future. Anything to escape from precarious balladry so difficult to cultivate sincerely as the saga age to which he belonged

in spirit sank further and further into the past! The censers he
swung over Springfield in his fantastic drawings were symbols of
his attempt to keep the religion of enthusiasm in a Middle West
slipping into mechanical mediocrity.

He revolted too against his own showmanship, but never while
he was at it. The chanting of his poems held audiences from
Oxford to Peoria, because, once launched upon the communal
chant, his heart rose up like the Psalmist's, and the coldest of
audiences was stirred. But the immense effort of recreating revival-
ism in a sophisticated scientific world wearied him, and his modern
self-consciousness was pricked by a half patronizing enthusiasm to
a realization that he was like the priestess of the Delphic Oracle
who was authentic only when a little intoxicated and perhaps
faintly absurd. He came a little late, and knew in his heart that
only one General Booth could enter heaven, and that the Congo
could not indefinitely boom. What could he do else—art, criticism,
or the movies?

And, indeed, now that he is dead we can say with honor that his
best is left behind him. He had the great good fortune to live all
of his poetic life within the years allotted to him. As with Poe,
there is room in an anthology for the best of his work, but that
best is inimitable.

Hazelton Spencer

The Life and Death of a Bard

When Vachel Lindsay died last December, worn out by the economic necessity of reciting "The Congo" to the nation's high-school kids, candidates for the bachelor's degree, and the nice boring people who frequent poetry societies, the American scene became the poorer, both as a show and in the loss of its chief poetical interpreter since Whitman. That is not saying that Lindsay was the greatest performer since Whitman, though I think he was. You can't rank the Twentieth Century Americans by a vertical scale unless you graduate it according to some definite conception of what you want from an American poet. We have with us always the dulcet warblers in Israel, the amiable obligers with epics by special request, the acidulous etchers, the stuntists, and, least deserving of respectful mention, the super-orthodox academic tortoises inching along well-worn trails. Trail-breakers and national star-reporters are not so common.

After the disappearance of Whitman and the New Englanders, American poetry lay in the doldrums. Lindsay had begun to write

From *American Mercury,* XXV (April 1932), 455-62. Reprinted by permission of *American Mercury.*

before the turn of the century, but no one knew about him or had heard of a New Poetry Movement till Harriet Monroe printed "General William Booth Enters Into Heaven" in *Poetry* for January, 1913. Then we learned that a new wind was blowing, and that one poet at least had been swept into an unploughed sea. Lindsay was the first to feel the breeze coming—that is a mere matter of dates—and as soon as he sniffed it he cracked on all sail. Of all the captains of the New Poetry Movement he was the real "driver" from first to last. Since that group revitalized the whole of American letters and gave our poetry the second of its great epochs—second chronologically but by no means certainly second in artistic achievement or social significance—his passing requires a salute from all who care about American art.

Lindsay's training for his unique function in the life of the Republic was not consciously undertaken with a poetic career in view. His suffering parents had little sympathy with his juvenile inclinations to artistic expression, which were at first directed less toward poetry than toward drawing, design, and painting—he studied at the Chicago Art Institute and later with Henri in New York. Still less were they pleased by his outspoken contempt for the smugly "Christian" and *bourgeois* standards of the Illinois town in which he was born and reared. The lover of Lindsay's verse who is unwise enough to visit Springfield will find the usual congeries of genially predatory State politicians, which gives it a slightly tarter flavor than most of the Main Streets, and there is of course the ever-green and ever-growing Lincoln legend there; but he will not be arrested by visible tokens of the reasons why Lindsay could write such lines as

> Let not our town be large, remembering
>   That little Athens was the Muses' home,
> That Oxford rules the heart of London
>   still,
>   That Florence gave the Renaissance to
>   Rome.

The mere juxtaposition of this prairie capital with those imperishable names has a grotesque effect on the visitor, till he recalls that Lindsay was a prophet and a bard, as critical in his way of the civilization that produced him as Sinclair Lewis has been in his. I am writing of Lindsay as I knew him and as he poured out his heart in numberless confidences which I have no intention of violating, at any rate not yet. But for anyone who can keep his feet against the knockdown surge of Lindsay's rhythms and the dazzling torrent of his imagery and allusions, his critical point of view is implicit in the poems.

II

Emerson thought of poets in two great classes, the versifiers and the bards. "For it is not metres, but a metre-making argument, that makes a poem—a thought so passionate and alive, that, like the spirit of a plant or an animal, it has an architecture of its own and adorns nature with a new thing."

Poe belongs with the former group, a magical spinner of shining and multicolored yarns, an artist in the sense that a versatile and infallible juggler is an artist, or a pitcher like Walter Johnson in his prime. Emerson and Whitman were bardic. That is why Emerson was one of the first to hail "Leaves of Grass." The dramatic poets, like Chaucer and Shakespeare, are not amenable to this classification because objectivity is indispensable to the painter who wants to fill a large canvas with sharply distinguished characters. But Milton was a bard and so was Wordsworth, and Browning, who, for all his powers of characterization, lacked the dramatist's detachment.

Now, you will not find in American poetry anything more stinging than "If the Red Slayer Think He Slays" or "Voluntaries," or more musical than "Out of the Cradle Endlessly Rocking"; but mere excitation or music-making is not enough to satisfy man's deepest poetic need. If it were, Herrick might stand beside Shelley, and "Helen, Thy Beauty Is to Me" or "Tears, Idle Tears" might be taken for great poetry. Sheer music-making is done better by the musicians than by the poets, just as opera handles romance on the stage better than drama does.

But the converse is also true. Does anyone seriously suppose that the finest measure in Beethoven, while it may move more people than, say, the final speech of the "Œdipos Tyrannos", can possibly move any one person as deeply as the most terrible speech of Sophocles, spoken at the close of a perfect production of the play, can move a thoroughly sensitive spectator? Both expressions, as sound and as exaltation, are titanic. But the summation of the greatest of all plays is charged with *thought*, to which even the most lofty page of pure music can never aspire. The intrinsic emotional content of both may be equal. But, in the case of the drama, as soon as thought comes into play the emotion is intensified to a point music cannot reach.

Moreover, the greatest poetry does not stop there:

> Unless to thought be added will,
> Apollo is an imbecile.

Thus Emerson, who was capable of incredible cacophony, but smote the bard's harp, not the lute, though he could subdue the former, on rare occasions, to a fine lyricism. It is not, then, their great lyric gifts alone that make his poetry and Whitman's so rich. There is a resistless power in it that sweeps us along with them because they are noble chanters much more than they are sweet singers. Where most poets tickle the ear pleasantly, they frequently stun, not always pleasantly, by the impact of their thought-laden, passion-driven lines. Their best stuff leaves you breathless and weak. Who drinks them burns his throat. The difference between Whitman at his best and Tennyson at his best is the difference between a shot of pre-War Haig and Haig and a perfectly engineered vanilla ice-cream soda.

Lindsay clearly belongs with Emerson and Whitman. None of his contemporaries, not even Yeats and Masefield, could write occasional single lines of more ravishing beauty than the poet of "The Chinese Nightingale," although so dominated were most of his readers and still more his auditors by the terrific vitality and racket of the great set-pieces that the more decorous poems were often ignored. If it is the sweet singers who give you chills up and down your spine (to borrow the æsthetic yardstick of the new chairman of the Metropolitan Opera), if you prefer the tootling flute, with Mr. Barrère most exquisitely and commendably kissing an air of Gluck (or Massenet) through his whiskers, to the full orchestra thundering Beethoven or Brahms, if you put Longfellow before Emerson, a Poe before a Whitman, you can find much in Lindsay that will please you but you are not likely to perceive that the charming little lyrics you approve of are quite of a piece with "Bryan, Bryan," "The Santa-Fé Trail," and "The Kallyope Yell." And you will certainly be disconcerted by the blunders that no one who loved the man this side idolatry would wisely attempt to explain away.

The major poets have to be forgiven appalling errors which the cautious minors never make. The man who lives or composes in constant apprehension of committing a breach of good taste may succeed in going to his grave with impeccable correctness or in writing a shelf of flawless verse. But he is not likely to have a very rich life; and, though his books may win him an honorable place as a minor poet, he will never be a great poet. It is desirable to revert to these truisms—they have been recognized as such since the days of Longinus—in reviewing the work of Vachel Lindsay. To the genuine bard every fragment of his art is a piece of his thought—even by-products are sparks from what Emerson called "the burning core below." To you or me they may seem ashes; we may wish the volcano had never spewed them up; we may even applaud the shivering rhymester who, standing at his domestic hearth, but more conscious of his audience than burning with his Idea, exhibits his artistic conscience and social tact by giving such productions to the only flame they have ever known.

God forbid that I should seem to insist on anyone's printing anything, to say nothing of everything. I am describing, not what ought to be, but what has been and is. A poet's poems are like an ordinary man's children: to hear a reflection on even the least attractive is unutterably wounding. There is much to be said for the craftsman who destroys an imperfect thing. But a reputation that rests more on the rejection of the imperfect than on the forthright, even if occasional and uneven, creation of the sublime, while it is one that merely talented men must rest content with, is not, in the eyes of an authentic artist, a reputation very much worth having. God is doubtless comforted by this reflection as He surveys the world He made. But the mortal artists whom I have observed at close range do not appear to derive much solace from it.

I heard once of a poet who boasted of the reams of never-to-be-published poetry that had gone up his study's fireplace. And a good thing too, no doubt. But he did not realize that he was giving his game away. Unfortunately, but in fact, the real bard seems rather to feel that all he writes is part of the record. He does not "release" his poems, as books, motion pictures, and interviews are said in the current jargon to be "released." He conjures them from the vasty deep, hammers them into publishable shape, and hurls them full in the face of the congregation. For the true bard considers his readers a sinful lot, desperately in need of his regenerating ministrations. "To believe that what is true for you is true for all men—that," said Emerson, "is genius." Lindsay belongs with the Yankee Merlin among those who exhort, prophesy, promulgate fearful curses, and play curious tricks with Gadarene and other breeds of this world's swine.

III

The New Poetry Movement was chiefly distinguished by the productions of six or eight highly remarkable poets. A slighter but no less real distinction resides in the appearance of scores if not hundreds of not so eminent but indubitably genuine poets, who put such pressure on the existing publishing mediums that little poetry magazines mushroomed up over-night throughout a land supposed to be indifferent to poetry. The N.P.M. was no Mexican army, and if we count the rank and file as well as the generals it is plain that the second great period of American poetry was incomparably the superior of the first. Even if we stick to the generals, though the margin decreases, the conclusion is probably similar.

As one star is held to differ from another star in glory as well as in magnitude, the chiefs of the N.P.M. differed. We are here of course more concerned with the nature of glories than with the extent of magnitudes. Miss Lowell was preëminently the critic of the whole affair. Not that her poems are to be minimized; a few of them seem likely to retain a permanent place in all anthologies of poetry in English. But she made her most effective contribution in her critical harangues and her gallant championing of the new styles.

Robinson hardly calls for mention. A survivor from the era of the poetic depression, he was less spiritually than chronologically a part of the Movement, and he is more the New Englander than the American anyway. So is Frost, who is the Whittier of the N.P.M., a poet of gentle genre studies rather than a voice of These States. Miss Millay, for pure concentrated passion perhaps the greatest poet who has yet appeared in this country, was never actually a part of the New Poetry group. Her art is timeless and unlocalized. She might as well have turned up in England as in America.

But there were three who could have appeared nowhere else. Perhaps the most remarkable single volume of the N.P.M. was "Spoon River"; but Masters remains a one-book man, though it is a very great book—both intrinsically and for its incalculable effect on subsequent American letters of every description. Nor did either he or Sandburg succeed in nationalizing themselves as Lindsay did. Sandburg seems consciously to have tried it in "Good Morning, America," but he is at his best when he deals with his Chicago's hog-butchery and the rootabagas of the adjacent plains.

To speak with the American voice a poet must be an all-American. Some of our most distinguished practitioners are as alien to parts of the continental United States as Masefield presumably is to, say, Bohemia or Sicily.

A terrifying hardship that confronts every artist in Mr. Hoover's America is the necessity of winning a national reputation, since a merely local one, unless achieved in New York, is not taken seriously except in a few of the most complacent cities of the Eastern seaboard, Boston and Baltimore, for example. The actual difference between the English and the American artist's plight may be grasped by a simple geographical comparison. It is easier for the new English genius to make himself known than for the new American genius. He has fewer miles to go.

Another physical handicap for the would-be all-American artist is the almost insurmountable difficulty of grasping the forty-eight Commonwealths and finding any unifying principle deeper than their common consumption of standardized, nationally advertised machinery, general merchandise, and light entertainment. With the possible exception of Mark Twain, no American writer of importance has ever geographically experienced the United States so thoroughly as Lindsay did. Even Whitman's adventures were less extended horizontally, though his thought, at least, ranged far up and down the elevator shaft of society.

Bound to escape his parents' determination to force him into the mold of the local Babbitts, Lindsay sadly thumbed his nose at the Springfield gods and took to the road. His wanderings are described in "Adventures While Preaching the Gospel of Beauty" and "A Handy Guide for Beggars." Sometimes he tackled the corner grocer on some little Main Street and offered to swap a broadside of his poetry for a tin of sardines. Sometimes he begged. His expeditions were renunciations and they were also austere and bitter protests. In the end he won, and no one dared gainsay his devotion of his life to art. Lindsay's tramping and begging corresponded in his inner life approximately to Whitman's abandonment of plug hat and frock coat in favor of flannel shirt and sombrero, and precisely to Emerson's resignation of his pulpit.

We who have nothing that would kill us if we did not say it, we whom fear holds back from the good life, who are we to sneer like M. Michaud at Emerson's blend of passionate idealism with Yankee common sense, like Professor Wendell at Whitman's sartorial gestures, like some contemporary Pharisees at Lindsay's occasionally uncouth gambolings or his tactless introduction of his

eccentric opinions into his poetry recitals? Lindsay was always at
white heat, intoxicated and boiling over with what a cool observer
could see was his own genius but he regarded as a Message. He
was an Ancient Mariner if there ever was one, and he held the
wedding guests in droves. Saul slew his thousands and David his
ten thousands, but Lindsay fixed them with his glittering eye and
recited, by modest computation, to at least a million auditors.
That alone was a stupendous achievement, probably never dupli-
cated in the history of poetry. It took its toll.

In this fat land, now getting a well-deserved taste of what most
of the world has always known, there was no one to stake its
greatest living poet to food and shelter. And so, though he was
burning to write new songs, Lindsay had to keep on the road all
his life, harder spurred than ever during the last few years by the
increasing needs of his family. Only now it was not the open road
of high adventure beside the springs of new creation; it was the
dreadful trail of the national lecturer. Back and forth from Maine
to California Lindsay drove himself, reciting, reciting, reciting—
shrinking from the crowds with a sensitiveness incredible to those
who did not know him—hoping with a childlike pathos that they
would accept him as well as his act—trying to preserve his temper
when silly committee-women insisted on hearing the old set-pieces
he had become so weary of performing.

Some day an artist will accept martyrdom for all his brethren
by rising and slaying the next person who demands the thing he
did years before and has repeated a thousand times. What does
Mr. Rachmaninoff think of the audience that will not go away till
he has played the C♯ minor prélude? I know what Lindsay thought
of the fools who had to be placated with "The Congo." It was iron
in his soul that he was required to pronounce on every platform
the thoughts he was thinking in 1912 instead of the new thoughts
he was thinking in 1930. If most of his recent poetry is inferior to
his earlier work, the decline must be attributed to the sapping of
his creative strength by his having to live by chanting and drama-
tizing instead of composing. He had never run dry, was still full
of ideas, and had a great deal he wanted to say about the contemporary circus. He had no desire whatever to lie back on his
past. The anti-saloon campaigner of the old days was still a Prohibitionist, but he was an ardent advocate of Al Smith in 1928.

The "road," then, was where Lindsay lived, and it seems indis-
putable that no other member of the N.P.M. had equal opportuni-

ties for laying his ear to the ground. He not only heard "the whisper of the prairie-fairies"—for his sensitiveness to Nature see "The Santa-Fé Trail"—but talked face to face, formally and informally, with all sorts and conditions of men from coast to coast. He knew the capitals well, but he never neglected the way-stations. I usually found him at least one jump ahead of the newspapers when it came to noticing political and social trends. All his colleagues of the N.P.M. were local reporters; Lindsay was a national star-reporter, with a sixth sense for being on the spot when the big news broke.

IV

Some of the journalistic obituaries laid great stress on his re-fusal to fly the house-flag of post-War pessimism that every so-phisticated artist is now supposed to nail to the masthead. There is no denying that Lindsay was an optimist. So were Emerson and Whitman. Much of the cheap depreciation of the former now current ignores his savagely critical attitude toward the pursy materialism of Nineteenth Century America. He saw no hope of destroying it, but he thought it might be harnessed for culture. Similarly, Whitman is derided for a simple faith in democracy by those who, never having read his prose, are ignorant that he was keenly aware of its failures, and that the political idealism of his poetry was a conscious protest against political reality.

Both Emerson and Whitman looked out upon a Republic highly cultivated in the agricultural, manufacturing, and commercial arts, and relatively uncultivated in the fine arts. Was their optimism about the latter's American future unwarranted? There is no evidence that America has yet saved her soul, and precious little that she has one to save. But both our literature and our fine arts now stand as high above their zenith when Emerson was fulminat-ing as the tall buildings of Al Smith's Manhattan do above the rathskellers of Bayard Taylor.

Now, the optimism of Vachel Lindsay was exactly the same brand as Emerson's and Whitman's. Like them he saw boundless possibilities in an American able to start at scratch, without the shackling handicaps of outworn European institutions and cults. His gospel of the New Localism was merely a more specific pre-scription for the same ills they prescribed for. Lindsay's Main Street, utopian as it may be, is certainly laid out on a more ra-tional programme than either Emerson or Whitman offered:

Now let each child be joined as to a church
To her perpetual hopes, each man ordained:
Let every street be made a reverent aisle
Where Music grows and Beauty is unchained.

At any rate, beauty *is* being unchained—wherever a specialist
in acquisition bequeaths his loot to a public art museum or a
library or an orchestra; or a park is laid out; or a campaign is won
against noise; or a monument is unveiled that is not a monstrosity;
or a contractor employs a real architect for a new row of houses; or
a public building turns out to be something more than a feat of
engineering.

The beauty of a materialistic civilization will never come out
of acquiescence, nor from the brushes of those artists who have
gone over to the enemy by trying to mechanize their work. If it
comes, it will be out of rebellion, and chiefly from conscious and
determined assaults by individuals on the depravity of the racke-
teers, standardizers, and advertisers, and on the inertia of the
politicians and boosters. If this is true, gentler souls must be willing to accept a little stridency in the voice of the American artist,
remembering that he purveys a man-made testament of beauty.
Where the natives sit back to contemplate the beauty of God as
expressed either in the wide open spaces or in the placid back-
waters of the East or South, the result is on the one hand that the
frantic mouthings of the Rotarians are confused with progress,
and on the other that the world is complacently allowed to go by
with only an occasional lynching to bear witness to the town's
spiritual alertness.

In the old *Village Magazine* these are the mottoes on the banners of the Village Improvement Parade:

Fair streets are better than silver; green parks are better than
gold.
Bad public taste is mob law; good public taste is democracy.
A crude administration is damned already.
A bad designer is to that extent a bad citizen.
Let the best moods of the people rule.
A hasty prosperity may be raw and absurd; considered poverty
may be exquisite.
Without an eager public all teaching is vain.
Our best pictures should be good painting; our best monuments
should be real sculpture; our best buildings should be real archi-
tecture.

Ugliness is a kind of misgovernment.
To begin, we must have a sense of humor and learn to smile.

Lindsay's optimism, then, was not the God's in His Heaven, all's right with the world variety. He was far too sensitive for that; he had suffered too much; he had been too lonely. Above all, he was too constantly in a state of rebellion, breathing fires and slaughters, and never was he, up to the last moment, really reconstructed. Such poems as "Three Hours" are statements of aspiration, not accomplishment:

> The moon was like a boat one night,
> And like a bowl of flowers;
> Three butterflies were riding there,
> Named for three lovely hours.
>
> The first hour was the hour the night
> Was a great dome of peace;
> The second hour was when the night
> Gave my heart release
>
> From all old grief and all lost love.
> And the third hour was when
> I found that I was reconciled
> To Heaven and Earth and men.

Lindsay could not feel that way very long at a time, not with the populace watching the Village Improvement Parade from the curb instead of joining it. There are a few socialist poems, but the tin-pot radical will not find a great deal of direct and vulgar denunciation of individuals in Lindsay's pages. He was too much the lover of a serene beauty for that, and he realized that conversion is not a matter of signing on the dotted line of a church or political party, but must come from within.

Here, again, he is like Emerson, who, regarding even the issue of Negro slavery as a minor and surface manifestation of a deep-rooted evil, did not leave it to the Southern orators to denounce alone the exploitation of the Northern wage-slaves. Beside his writings, and the best of Whitman's, stand Lindsay's, to point the unpleasant contrast between the America that might be and the America that is.

V

In the introduction to his "Selected Poems" I enlarged upon Lindsay's lyric gifts because they had been neglected in critical discussions of his poetry. They were of the highest order, as those who heard him chant "The Chinese Nightingale" well know. My suggestion that the poet's vocal performances ought to be preserved met with general approval, and thanks to the zeal of Professor Cabell Greet the library of Columbia University now contains records of slightly more than half the book. I now offer the further suggestion that some phonograph company proceed to make them commercially available. A market awaits them in the schools, as well as among poetry lovers in general.

The records were made only in the nick of time; but they were made, and the voice survives the bard. There is no use, I suppose, in speculating about the poems he wanted to write. After an interim, during which it looked as though Lindsay were through, he seemed to have caught his second wind and become again the incarnation of creative vitality. He was one of the most alive things I have ever had dealings with, so fiercely alive that I find it even now hard to accept his death as real. But that terrific energy had to be applied to the recitals instead of to composition. To do both meant shouldering a double load. Whether he could have sustained it is doubtful. The old rhetorical pieces demanded by recital audiences kept his vocalizing in a groove that led away from the kind of music he wanted to make. He was himself fully aware of his predicament and faced it for the most part courageously; but he was sometimes profoundly depressed by it, and the consequent strain undoubtedly contributed to his death at fifty-two.

No man ever loved the American people more than Vachel Lindsay did, and no man ever had a loftier vision of his country or tried harder to help his fellow-citizens realize it. But his death was front-page news because he was known as a jazz poet, and because when he harangued the poetry circles about his deepest convictions, they seemed and he seemed a motley to the view.

Henry Morton Robinson

The Ordeal of Vachel Lindsay
A Critical Reconstruction

In the autumn of 1909 a curious booklet appeared in Springfield, Illinois. It was entitled *The Tramp's Excuse*, and the author
—a thirty-year-old art student just returning from New York to
his native town—went broke publishing it. But no matter; he was
to go broke many times publishing just such pamphlets and he
did not lack courage to begin. The innocent nudes in *The Tramp's
Excuse* shocked the town and caused the author to lose his job as
art lecturer in the local Y. M. C. A. But again, no matter. For
Vachel Lindsay, author and illustrator of the little volume, had
set down as its frontispiece the chart of his being, a pen and ink
drawing entitled "A Map of the Universe".

Fifteen years later he wrote in the foreword to his *Collected
Poems*: "The Map has dominated all my verses".

The "Map" is a bizarre and fantastic jumble of *Edda* symbolism, Egyptian design, and Swedenborgian mysticism, difficult to
describe and impossible to understand. It depicts Heaven and
Earth and the vast interstellar spaces crowded with symbols that
must have had special meanings to Lindsay, meanings that even

From *The Bookman,* LXXV (April 1932), 6-9.

he could not wholly grasp or interpret either by verbal or graphic means. Commenting on one of the symbols, the Amaranth Vine, he says: "Under the walls of Heaven we see the Amaranth Vine growing from Earth to Heaven. This is but a diagram of the Vine, not a picture. The picture it is impossible to draw. None of the pictures are possible to draw". As with the Amaranth Vine, so with the Tomb of Lucifer, the Spider of Mammon, and the Tree of Laughing Bells,—vague symbols all, symbols of something that Lindsay never made quite clear to himself or anyone else.

The total effect of the "Map" is one of undigested fantasy, devoid of graphic or metaphysical unity, possessing none of the dark madness of Blake, but suggesting instead that the artist had a double touch of puerility: first, to compose such a drawing; and second, to lay such prodigious store by it. And yet Lindsay speaks of this Map in every sentence of his discourse, places it at the head of his *Collected Works*, and exhorts us to bear it constantly in mind while reading his verses. Such emphasis must not be allowed to pass unregarded. Quite probably the Map is the clue to the poet's recurrent protest, uttered before a thousand audiences, "I don't want to recite *The Congo;* you can recite it as well as I can. I don't want to recite *General Booth Enters into Heaven.* I want to talk about the Queen of Bubbles, the Amaranth Vine, and the Twenty-Six Panels of the Village Improvement Parade". Of course he always *did* go on and chant *The Congo* and *General Booth,* and then let off his *Kallyope Yell* with all the amazing effects of his loud and marvellous voice. For these performances he was justly famous; by them he will be remembered in the hearts of grateful hearers. But during the last fifteen years of his life his early poems irked and thwarted him terribly, and if we are to understand his growing irritation with audiences that demanded them, we must heed the poet's advice and scrutinize more carefully his hieroglyphic Map of the Universe.

It will reveal to us a truth about Vachel Lindsay that is not to be found in facile summaries of his hoboing experiences, his picturesque roadside recitals, or his later successes on the lecture platform. Like Mark Twain, Lindsay went through an ordeal which he himself helped to create and foster, yet which at the same time he dreaded and despised. Audiences expected Mark Twain to be comical when he desired above all things to be speculatively philosophic. Similarly, American audiences begged Vachel Lindsay to electrify them with his delivery of *The Santa Fé Trail* when he himself wanted to discourse upon his Map of the Universe and how it all tied up with Egyptian hieroglyphics and Springfield City Hall. Naturally there was a polite but determined lack of interest in the audience when Lindsay began to unreel his mystical cosmology, and I cannot help feeling that this lack of interest was quite justified. On these matters Lindsay was dull, unimpressive; but when he got down to the business of declaiming his own poetry he was dynamic and unforgettable. I once heard him expound some of his Egyptian lore to a group of writers and teachers at Columbia University. At 9 p.m. Lindsay began his exegesis of the hieroglyphic Map; at 10.30 he was still droning on —but to a roomful of empty chairs. Unable to support the weight of his discourse, two-thirds of the audience had slunk out for a smoke. But when they heard the first "boomlay" beats of *The Congo* they rushed back to listen, applaud, and clamour for more. Swedenborg, Confucius and Thoth they could get elsewhere; what they wanted from Lindsay was the good old Mumbo-Jumbo, Sizz-Fizz, and Boomlay-BOOM.

Since humour was not a part of Vachel Lindsay's make-up, he was unable to be good-tempered about this thrice-evident truth. He grew progressively sourer with his audiences, and could not bring himself to realize that they had paid their money to hear a great modern jongleur thump out his own syncopated rhythms. He refused to see that America had made a myth of him, based on its first vision of the tawny-haired young poet springing full-grown from the Chicago movement of 1912. At first he could not realize that his best work and his best manner were irrevocably hurled forth in that year. No man likes to believe that his great days are behind him. He may fear it, and unconsciously resent it. But admit it? Never! He may even attempt a new synthesis, but usually the earlier mould has set, and the public will not let him break it. Unless he is a major force, capable of limitless expansion (and after 1915 Lindsay was not a highly-energized poet), he is hearsed in a tight category and swathed in cerements of his own winding.

This, I believe, was Vachel Lindsay's tragedy: As a fairly young man he made a reputation for himself by declaiming his highly-accented and dramatically original poems; as time passed he grew tired of these poems (imagine the monotony of reciting *The Congo* five thousand times!) and naturally wished to write something better. But he was unable to write anything better, and even if he had been, it is doubtful that his audience would have listened to it. And so he found himself approaching fifty, and passing it, obliged to do the same thing that he had done twenty years ago, but without freshness or savour now—no longer a poet of promise, no longer a poet at all—merely a touring performer compelled to revive for hire the painful memories of his poetic youth. No wonder he sought refuge in hieroglyphic mysticism!

II

Vachel Lindsay was a poet with a physical pulse of rhythm swelling like a life-tide within him. He was a *pulse*, and a pulse exclusively. He could not think profoundly or connectedly, and the emotional range of his poetry is limited to a few notes. As long as he could translate his poetic impulses into almost purely rhythmical terms he was regarded, and rightly, as one of the leaders of the new poetry. Before Lindsay's voice was heard, the pulse of American poetry beating through the scholarly arteries of Clarence Stedman and George Edward Woodberry, was thin and fluttery. Lindsay supplied an elastic bass-drum heart that sent it tumbling along its courses with new vigour. Poems like *The Golden Whales of California* and *The Booker Washington Trilogy* were like strong meat to readers dieted on the fragile cates of Hovey and Le Gallienne. Lindsay's violent rhythms gave a fillip to any subject matter, especially when volleyed forth double-forte by a powerful young man with golden hair and a crusader's magnetism in his throat. More than any poet of his day Lindsay kindled in the public a desire to hear poetry uttered by its maker; he excelled all his contemporaries—Amy Lowell, Alfred Kreymborg, Robert Frost and Carl Sandburg (compelling personalities all)—in the art of putting a poem across. In fact he put his poems across so convincingly that those who heard him cannot tell to this day whether it was the poetry or the delivery that was touched by greatness.

Then, after a period of elocutionary success, came the necessity of going on. But for Lindsay there was no place to go. His characteristic poems were already written; his emotions had not deepened; and his intellect, never profound or penetrating, was unable to plunge beneath the rippling muscle-sheath of rhythm that, for him, overlay reality. Meanwhile his critical environment was the reverse of stimulating; was he not one of Miss Monroe's poets, and could *they* do wrong? Not, at any rate, in Springfield or Chicago. Acclamation had done its work with such unfortunate results that Lindsay began to feel that whatever he sang or said was a glowing fragment of the *Logos*. Moreover, he had by this time acquired a pose that, for a while at least, was very pleasant to assume—the pose of a lusty jongleur-vagabond with a kind of picaresque tramping-on-life philosophy that has ruined better poets than Harry Kemp.

Into this situation, already fatal to poetic expansion, stalked the blight of Lindsay's strange tendencies towards hieroglyphia, a malady which in Lindsay's case closely resembled automatic writing. With his imagination depleted and his store of poetic energy uncomfortably low, Lindsay fell back upon fantasy, civic virtue, and the graphic arts—a trilogy that led him far from the paths of poetry in his declining years. He would take a pen and make scrolls such as one might make while holding a telephone receiver; the hieroglyphics thus produced were highly valued by him, both as drawings and as the graphic incubators of his verse. Speaking of his creative impulsion, he says: "I begin with hieroglyphic, the minute cell of our thoughts, the very definite alphabet with which we are to spell out our great new vision". Doubtless he stimulated his own creative impulse by tracing these hieroglyphs, and to this extent they serve a legitimate and valid purpose in his life. No one cares what a poet does as long as he produces poetry. He may affect intimacies with Buddha, Mencius, and Henry George —and while he is throwing off poems like *The Chinese Nightingale* and *The Golden Whales* he is immune from the petty darts of criticism. It is only when his work becomes attenuated, or hag-ridden by some semi-mystic theory that critics have a right to lament. And so I lament now that Vachel Lindsay, who in his towering prime was a signal-blaze to American poetry, spent the last fifteen years of his life in the service of hieroglyphic nonsense, arguing with audiences that his poems should be drawn, and danced, but never sung; lecturing in a very special jargon upon his hieroglyphic sketches of the Sun and Moon; and descanting always upon the interrelations of sign-writing and the millennium. If you want an adventure in jargonese, read Lindsay's own preface to his *Collected Works*. It is a pitifully rambling piece of prose containing not a word about the poems on which his fame rests— poems that he could not duplicate or even approach during the last years of his life. The Preface suggests, better than anything else, the ordeal through which the poet passed during those years —an ordeal which he had neither the strength to renounce nor the ability to transcend.

But let the note of querulous lamentation fade now, and all but the voice of ungrudging admiration be still. For when the critical score is balanced, it will be found that Vachel Lindsay has at least six poems in the small chaste urn containing all that one age passes on to the next. The pieces he will be remembered by (if I may venture into the dangerous realm of prophecy) are: *The Chinese Nightingale, The Congo, The Santa Fé Trail, General William Booth Enters into Heaven, The Golden Whales of California,* and the exquisite tribute to Altgeld, *The Eagle That is Forgotten.* Six such poems are enough. Enough to fill most of us with enduring gratitude and not a few of us with incurable envy. These poems are rigged with a vitality that was new in 1912 and is still new in 1932. With energy undiminished, and not a trace of barnacle to mar their glittering hulls or retard their swooping speed, they bound forward like clipper ships running before a live gale. That they will safely make the harbour of a secure immortality is not to be doubted by anyone who has watched their gait and direction for the past twenty years.

That America has a way of ordealizing its heroes by idealizing them is tragically apparent in the case of Vachel Lindsay. For at least ten years he came nearer to being our Hero as Poet than any man since Walt Whitman. Accordingly we placed him on a very high and very special pedestal, and demanded only of him that he remain where we placed him. That he wished to get down, move around, and go forward if possible, made no difference to us. We had "niched" him and we kept him niched, with all the implications good and bad of that elevating process. And now, rereading the great poems that he wrote before we made him an idol, it seems a trifle absurd, rather cheaply patronizing, to pity this man. Yet we do pity him; not for what he was, or what he failed to be, but for the writhing ordeal he must have undergone during the last years of his life.

Edgar Lee Masters

The Tragedy of Vachel Lindsay

With Lindsay's celebrity, which came with the publication of his poem on General William Booth, and had been prepared for by the publication of three poems in the Fall of 1912 in New York magazines, that life of study and solitary rumination ended which he had led since his youthful days at Hiram College.

He had struggled fiercely to free himself from a shell of incubation, and had wounded himself trying to do so. Now he was emancipated from the obscurity and the impotence that had cramped his being before. He had something to do to occupy his energies beside introspection and planning, though unfortunately he never ceased either of these. He became a platform celebrity as well as a famous poet, and instead of hearing the windmills afar as he tramped along the Santa Fé trail, he heard the nerve-wracking clicking of Pullman wheels; instead of livery-stables and old sheds in which to sleep on a bed of charity he had hotel rooms amid the racket of cities; and instead of sleeping like a stone after a day of walking in the open air, he often tossed with his head

From *American Mercury*, XXIX (July 1933), 357-69. Reprinted by permission of *American Mercury*.

53

full of blood, and his heart beating from an evening of reciting "The Congo" and "The Chinese Nightingale." Instead of the song of the Rachel Jane along the hedges of Kansas, he had the iterant questions and nervous giggling of club women in the Middle West, and everywhere over America. All this until his nerves ran blood. No more would he walk from Tampa to Richmond, Ky.; from New York City to Hiram, O.; from Springfield, Ill., to New Mexico. His *Lehrjahre* and his *Wanderjahre* were both over.

His last diaries are full of irritable and querulous exclamations. "I have been highbrowed to death. I have heard enough tall talk to build ten thousand towers of Babel." Everywhere he went he was asked the same set of questions. "I hunger and thirst for a new set." Lindsay had dignity both natural and acquired, but he was also democratic of manner, and quite accessible. On the lecture circuit hand-shaking, autographing, and some dining-out were inevitable. He had burned ten thousand candles, and read rooms full of books, dreaming utopias and his own mastership of the domains of religion and art, and the regeneration of America. It had all come to lecturing, in the face of sworn resolutions that he would never waste himself in any such way.

His diaries are full of ultimatums. He would be an artist with a new art, and thus dominate his city and his State and America; he would be a Christian cartoonist, and thus purify the politics of his country; he would be an art critic and make or mar the fortunes of artists. But to be a lecturer, that he would never be! And here he had become one; and having a genuine gift for the business, equal to that of James Whitcomb Riley, and greater than that of any contemporary American or Englishman, he was greatly in demand. His world-conquering programmes were cherished with an intensity of preoccupation which was nothing short of megalomanic. However, when he stepped at last into a place of power, where he could measurably influence the culture of his time, he found that the fatigues of travel and the vexations of the platform robbed him of peace, of the capacity to write, and of health and strength.

Lecturing was a way to live, but though his fees were good, they were not comparable to those of Mr. Masefield, and the other English authors who have a clever way of selling themselves to America, and a free way of making fun of the golden goose which they pluck when they have the mind. No one in the England of his time could compare to Lindsay as a recitationist; and yet, though he might believe in America and her future, and fall to his knees in adoration of republican institutions, he had to face the fact that Mr. Masefield could come to Illinois, to Chicago, and there draw twice over what Lindsay's own fees were for telling a presentably cultured audience about the plots and characters of Shakespeare's plays. This was true all over America.

On top of it Lindsay discovered to his woe that there was a deadly parasitism in the lecture business by which lecture agencies get the fat and leave the rind to the lecturer. Like his mother, however, he lived by forensic excitement, by agitation, and by the activity of that egotism which he confessed he had. At bottom, all this may reveal nothing but a Puritan tampering with life, a kind of fidgety dabbling with the universe, in order that life may be made over in the likeness of the desire of one feeble human mind. It may be, in fact, only an excess of thyroid. At all events, it is the basic chemical which makes tyrannicides, revolutionists, zealots and founders of religions, and writers of Golden Books of Springfield.

Thus Lindsay ceased to live for the sake of living, for his thoughts and his perceptions, as Thoreau lived. No business man slaving at his desk was more chained down than he was as he traveled all over America again and again, reciting his poems until he could say that more than a million people had heard him. And all this for the mere means of life! He could study an Egyptian grammar in order to draw hieroglyphics, but he failed to take to heart what Emerson said, namely, that "the strength of the Egyptian is to sit still." The touring cars went clacking and quacking in mad haste to get somewhere, and Lindsay sang the folly of such empty activity, but he himself came hastening from the Atlantic to the Pacific—and just for bread, not cake.

He could even observe that in all the cities of America there is nothing but streets for the hastening multitudes, no chairs on the sidewalks, no cafés in which to rest, no place to sit down and enjoy life. But though noting this fact, so significant of America's conception of order and law and the good life, he too ran on, and found no rest except in hotels, where he recuperated for the next day's ordeal. He had sworn himself to beggary and the road, to St. Francis as his patron saint, to Johnny Appleseed as his exemplar; and he became a lecturer; and even so, poverty dogged him and overtook him. His helmet was not the tin pan of Johnny Appleseed, but a cluster of flies about his bleeding forehead.

Would he have written more and better poems if he had lived for
the sake of life itself? Perhaps not; and so we may refrain from
wishing that we might have remade him.

II

In 1920 Lindsay made his first really national tour as a platform poet. In that year he had published "The Golden Whales of
California, and Other Poems in the American Language," which
had been loudly ridiculed. For that matter, even "The Chinese
Nightingale and Other Poems" had been sharply attacked by one
of the New York poets in the Chicago *Daily News*, a medium that
had a great circulation in Springfield. Thus he was facing the
ordeal of keeping his spirit clear and his nerves fresh in the face
of ridicule, and while traveling and lecturing.

Lindsay sang naturally or not at all. Criticism only made him
self-conscious; it only hurt the sale of his books, and lowered his
vitality. Thus at this time, when he was just forty, the shadows
dropped about him on every side, and he began to see himself as
a mere figurante of the times, whose vogue was passing, and had
even passed. All this despite his enormous egotism, which he
asserted in self-defense at this period, but vainly enough. His ex-
tensive reading at the Art Institute at Chicago, and at Hiram
College, and his thorough study of Milton and other heroic poets,
had laid a very considerable foundation for a lifetime's work—too
broad indeed for his powers, gnawed as they were by congenital
weakness of mind and body; and so now the material which he
had gathered for poems began to liquefy, to escape as mist, to
vanish out of his control.

However, in this year a happy experience came to him, and one
which extended his fame and gave him courage. In August he
went to England accompanied by his mother, where he was hospitably received in London and at Oxford. "My word, what a
man!" said the English, who had been excited by the colloquialisms of "The Everlasting Mercy." Lindsay was cordially entertained by John Masefield and other notables. On one occasion he
received a guinea for a recital; for the rest he exchanged rhymes
for tea and cakes, instead of for bread, as on the tramp to New
Mexico in 1912. English lecturers at Chicago used to refuse to go
on the platform until their honoraria were handed them, but
Lindsay, as the pilgrim boy, "lame but hunting the shrine," seemed
satisfied. For one thing, when he returned to Springfield in No-

vember with the glamour of English recognition clinging to him, that was much; for, above all, he craved the acclaim of his home town.

It now looked as if after long years, after the days of 1909, of the War Bulletins in favor of utopias and Christ and grape juice and chastity, and the disturbing effect of those feuilletons upon his standing in the community, he had captured his people, and could abide in their midst as an honored citizen, a supported institution. But it was not to be so. A banquet was given him and his mother, at which, according to the report of one present, Lindsay betrayed a pride in his English conquest which seemed invidious to the Springfield audience. According to the same witness, Mrs. Lindsay measurably mollified its resentment by a charming talk, worthy of a finished politician in a tight place. Nevertheless, Springfield, which had seemed to open its arms, folded them and stared at Lindsay and turned from him.

He was again on the long, long road, not watching the clouds above the wheat fields of Kansas, and hearing the Rachel Jane, but looking at the country from a Pullman window. For the most part this was true for the rest of his life, making exception of the tramp which he took with Stephen Graham in 1922 through Glacier Park. While he was on that tramp Lindsay's mother died. This was the disruption of his whole universe. Even a wholly masculine man will feel that the death of his mother severs a spiritual umbilical cord, and sets him apart to live an independent existence, where he must sustain himself as he can. As for Lindsay, who never grew up, whose mother had been his stay even when he disliked and feared her, and his nourishment, his bosom of rest when he loved her, he was struck down into confusion and darkness when this tragedy befell him. He suffered in consequence a complete nervous and physical collapse. In spite of his rugged appearance, he was not a robust man; he was a man of nerves, of inherited pathologies.

Fast following upon the death of his mother came the legal business of settling her estate. Philistine Springfield now saw its opportunity to get rid of Lindsay. He loved the old Lindsay home, he had chosen Springfield for his own for life, but now an artificial disagreement was fomented between him and his sisters, by which he lost the occupancy of the house. Thus his ancestral abode was turned into a boarding-house, and he wandered off. The old heirlooms were locked in the closet, the miniatures of the Nicholases and the Vachels were huddled in drawers, and what Lindsay called

"the fat, rich, illiterate, climacteric women of Springfield" rejoiced
as they kept well disposed heirs on the warpath by a cross fire of
"financial advice."

The house became a sort of show place where visitors were
conducted to the room where Lindsay wrote and drew. "All the
fat females who were so lustful of useless power, who brought
this about, not one of them willingly opened a book in her life."
So wrote Lindsay to me from Spokane in 1927 by way of show-
ing that he appreciated the trying experiences which I had gone
through, and was going through at the time, not dissimilar in
substance to his own. Considering that he was the only person
of the name who had ever achieved anything in life, and that his
work gave the only distinction to the name which it had, and also
that he was not fitted to cope with the world and to make a
living for himself, and that his sisters were married and in comfortable state, he should have inherited the house *in toto*, and
thus have been placed beyond the reach of legal attack. Christian
mothers and fathers spend their seventy years and more talking
of morals and Heaven and righteousness, and yet when they come
to any practical justice, like the matter of disposing of their
possessions, they often fall down completely.

What should Lindsay do now? He thought of going back to the
Chicago Art Institute, and there enrolling for another year. He
would thus commence all over, as if he were twenty-one years old.
In moments of flush blood he confessed that he was vain, egotisti-
cal, and as conceited as a turkey cock. "Just plain, colloquial
conceit is the word that describes me. Egoism and megalomania
are entirely too lofty." But, nursing his critical wounds, he de-
scended to vast humilities. "I do not want to be asking the
humblest place as a poet. The only words that ever cheer me up
are bard, ballad singer, troubadour." He was also planning, theo-
rizing and dreaming as of old; but in a stranger way, perhaps, than
ever. In his eighty-fifth year he wanted to be a Senator well
known for his drawings. He even thought of running for Congress.
Again he looked forward to his one hundredth and one hundred
and fifth years, when he would be producing drawings based on
Chinese script and Egyptian hieroglyphics.

In this bewildered state of mind he went to Gulfport, Miss., in
the Spring of 1923, where he became a resident poet at Gulf Park
College. That was one of the fashionable prescriptions of the day,
as the result of the Poetry Revival of 1914. But Lindsay's experiences at Gulf Park only added to his misfortunes. He did not

please the authorities of the college, and they greatly displeased him. His work was not congenial, and it was complicated by a romance which the college authorities presumed to disfavor, and which the object of his interest did not reciprocate.

Lindsay's love-life is reticently concealed in his papers and diaries. But the facts are that while at Hiram in 1904 he became engaged to a Springfield woman and the engagement lasted for several years. When he saw that he could not, for money reasons, marry this woman, he asked to be released, and he was released. In the beginning of his fame he devoted himself to another woman, but she could not see him in a marriageable light, and so married another. Lindsay dreamed of love all his life, and his Eve poems and others are full of passion. All the while he remained a virgin and was very proud of the fact. As a little boy his father had terrified him with talk of venereal disease, and this fear, coupled with religious scruples, kept him on a lonely path where he was miserable enough, even to nervous disturbances and physical ills which were the result of his celibacy. On the other hand, he never had many temptations to lapses. He was not attractive to women, first because of his moral austerities, and second, because his manner was self-consciously histrionic, and lacked the simplicity which guarantees comradeship and understanding.

When he went to Gulf Park he was but forty-four, which is to say, he was at an age when many men are youths in body, and men in minds, and for this double power are irresistible magnets to women of understanding. At this time he had celebrity, which in a place like Gulf Park may have been even awe-inspiring. But this did not overcome his lack of emotional attraction. Lonely and grieving, half discouraged and growing more afraid of the desolate years crowding upon him, hungering for affection, for comradeship and understanding, he was altogether in the most sensitive state that it is possible for a human being to be in.

Thus fated, he met with an admirable woman still in her early twenties, and his heart flamed with an intense and subtle fire. She did not return his passion, and did not consider him at any time as a possible husband. Many young women would have been flattered to death by this court paid by a celebrity, and they would have led Lindsay on, drinking his heart's blood like a Clarimonde, but flying from him when he was completely fooled and had nothing more to give. The young woman in question behaved toward him with the most perfect honesty and frankness; she indulged in no coquetry, she told him from the first in the most straightforward way that she felt no emotion for him, and never could feel any.

Lindsay was hurt; but the matter is less important than other things which bear upon his tragedy. The malapert intermeddling of a relative embarrassed him with the college authorities. Though there was no romance on the woman's part to rupture, his devotion was made the occasion for this presumptuous interference, which disturbed his position in the school. In Lindsay's state of health and mind this blow from a quarter where he had the right to expect good will and good judgment in his behalf was humiliating to the last degree, and helped to stagger his insecure psychology.

It must be said to his credit,—indeed, it cannot be overstated —that he was a generous heart, a fair mind. Despite his training and his heredity, and his intense prepossessions, he said farewell more than once without bitterness; more than once he kept the memory of lost loves in chivalrous and tender memory, without any resentment. What is more important, he overcame many weaknesses to be a joyous and hopeful singer. He had as much reason to take to drink as Burns or Poe had. He could have turned to misanthropy with as much justification as Byron did. But though he was not a great power like many poets who could be mentioned, he behaved like one in these exigencies, when his towering imagination was threatening his thinking and clouding his vision. His production as a poet cannot be fully appraised without taking into account the difficulties, external and internal, with which he bravely coped.

III

But this was not all of the Gulf Park crisis. The most poisonous arrow which had entered him by now was the growing sense that he could less frequently transcend himself, as he had done in such poems as "The Chinese Nightingale", that his material came less plastically and manageably to his hands. He accepted this defeated romance as evidence that his powers were waning, else he would not have been rejected, a false conclusion but a natural one in the state of his lowered self-confidence. In this condition of affairs he wandered on, this time to Spokane.

It was the Spring of 1924. He gave no hint that he would not return, but that was his purpose. He felt that his plans at Gulf Park were thwarted, that they wanted to make him a routine teacher, which was contrary to the understanding. He felt that he was isolated, that he was not appreciated, that his books were not read there, nor was any attempt made to have them read. He said that no one read his books from Gulf Park to New Orleans. He was burying loyalties to his art, and to his writing in the thankless duties of the school. He was unhappy about his mother's death, and depressed about his isolation and the failure of his influence as a resident poet.

But when he got to Spokane all was changed. There he found Percy Grainger, the composer. His hotel rooms became an artistic center. He began to write again, and to chant and sing at the nearby colleges. His spiritual nostrils inhaled reviving oxygen; and in this situation he decided to make Spokane his home and to return no more to Gulf Park. When he disclosed his intention to the school authorities there, they accused him of a breach of contract, but he argued out the matter with them, and adhered to his purpose to stay in the fascinating Northwest, where he had found attention and friendship of the kind that were honorable to his position in life.

After he had been in Spokane about a year he met Elizabeth Conner again, whom he had first seen in 1912 at Mills College, when he was returning to Springfield from the tramp of that year. She was then a little girl; now she was a woman of about twenty-five. She had been well educated; she was devoted to poetry and wrote it skillfully; she was well read in many literatures; but above all, she was a woman of fine breeding, of lively spirits, of sanguine vitality, of a fine integrity of mind and heart. She was variously trained and equipped to be the wife of a poet, and no other woman of Lindsay's life was so well fitted to fill the difficult rôle which she undertook with a brave heart and a devoted spirit. Thus it was that he had this interest to keep him in Spokane for the time. They were married on May 19, 1925, and tramped as a honeymoon excursion through Glacier Park, where Lindsay wrote many poems, some of the most musical and poignant of his whole life.

But Spokane was not the utopia which he had dreamed it was. Lindsay declared in letters that Spokane had invited him to be its guest while the Springfield estate was being settled and during this period of mourning for his mother. He discovered that he was a paying guest, and the millionaires there gave him to understand that he was to do something for their hospitality. They suggested that he might be made a special writer on one of the morning papers, if he proved to be tractable. They hinted that he should emulate the work of Eddie Guest and not play highbrow any more. They enjoined upon him that he cease his eccentricities, change his church to the Episcopalian, write up the president of the Greeters' Association, regulate the number of his children according to their ideas, put himself at the disposal of no one worth less than a million dollars, write poems on William Waldorf Astor instead of on Andrew Jackson, and turn himself from a Jefferson Democrat into a Tory Republican. When he didn't and wouldn't do these things he discovered that the hospitality of Spokane was counterfeit. Stories were started on him that he was affluent, and wouldn't pay his bills, that he was subsidized by a railroad, that he and his wife were in disharmony and had started to be divorced. Such are the charges which Lindsay made against Spokane in letters written by him at this time. He said:

> I am certainly a citizen of Springfield, and will be till I die. I want to get back there as soon as possible, to my birthplace with my wife and children, and stay there forever. I see no reason why I should be banished like Dante, and heckled by strangers. They heckle me and then say "Isn't it sad?" These are the things that keep me from being the singer that I once was. I want to sing and I want a place to sing. Why should the room where I once wrote be exhibited as a commercial curiosity, while I have to fight for the chance to live there? It is like cutting off the leg of a perfectly well man, and then exhibiting it in alcohol in a museum. They all expect me to be as good a lawyer as Elihu Root, and as good a poet as Homer twenty-four hours of the day, or else to take the consequences. And how they love to break me, and then try to pity me!

And so in the Spring of 1929 he returned with his family to Springfield. He had been lecturing while at Spokane, and he continued to do so now. He was nearing fifty, and needed honor, love, troops of friends. He had none of them. If Philistine Americans withhold their support and friendship from the radicals in literature, upon what ground did they deny them to Lindsay the conformist? During these years he had frequently passed through Springfield, looking longingly at the old scenes. But he wanted to return there as a conqueror, and he tried to dramatize such an entrance, with results soon to be shown.

Illinois, like the other States, has always been devoured and ridden by bureaucrats, by parasites, by poseurs and patriots, by

Cagliostros of all causes. In Chicago there were firemen's pension funds for those who sprinkled water on houses afire. There were municipal employés' annuities to feed those who carried elections, and got jobs thereby, and then fed at the public trough for years. There were park employés' annuities, and policemen's annuities, and annuities for employés of the public libraries, for those who handed books from shelves, Lindsay's included. There were teachers' pensions. Illinois had given purses to the widows of dead Governors, and Governors, at that, who had betrayed the State and civilization.

Lindsay was greater than any Governor, and he had spent his life trying to enrich and ennoble his State, not to impoverish and degrade it. Illinois could have honored itself by granting him a life pension of $150 a month. In that way he might have returned as a conqueror to his old home. Instead he entered Springfield only to start forth again on the soul-exhausting lecture platform, where a stereotyped demand for "The Congo" compelled him to recite it until he trembled from head to foot with revulsion when he heard the title spoken. Illinois's wealth was $22,000,000,000 at the time; Chicago was full of millionaires; Springfield had many too; and some of these had made their money by exploiting and stealing the resources of the State, and by operating mills of ignorance and calumny. They had thriven on the fame of Lindsay. But prayers and editorials and wreaths are cheaper than pensions, and make as much noise.

IV

His years of lecturing while at Spokane and after he returned to Springfield may be considered together for their bearing upon his failing powers, and the evidence of failure as shown by his letters and diaries. He often wrote to his wife in words which tragically told the impact which fatigue and dispraise, and the lessening interest in his work, were making upon his vitality. His was a centrifugal nature, expansive and discursive, and therefore lyrical. As he went on and the centrifugal forces in him increased under the relaxed check of languor and self-pity, these forces became wild flames at times, flames of spurts and flares, which were no longer the steady fire of the crucible. Lindsay strove to acquire a good prose style, and at times he wrote prose of tolerable merit. His poetry is rarely distinguished by really magical words, by the one word which opens up vistas of vision like look-

ing through a fieldglass. But in this bewilderment of his mind his
prose now became verbose, and his poetry spread out like a stream
in a swamp, without direction, without a current, full of sediment
and floating stuff.

His habitual ideas, such as magical Springfield, cathedrals, the
Virgin Mary, the bringing in of a new era of music, poetry, liberty
for America, became less like the speculations of Swedenborg, and
more like the Cumorah visions of Joseph Smith, or the hallucina-
tions of Mohammed in the cave of Mount Hira. Yet he could still
write in this admirable way:

> I see this whole land as a unit. I have traveled over it so much,
> and a thousand songs and drawings have almost reached the sur-
> face about it. . . . I seem to have a kind of heartache for every
> State in the Union, no matter how silly that may seem. I love the
> United States, and in spite of all the struggle of this tour I love
> the land that I have passed over. Every morning from the train
> has been lovely.

Whitman never said anything more heartfelt, more devotional
to America. But both struggled in vain to express their love.
Sometimes Lindsay seemed to capture his vision by apostrophes
to the Republic of Jefferson, as Whitman sang an America rising
free from every species of Toryism to the heights of new life for
a new race. But neither ever captured the central idea solvent of
the whole, and in Lindsay's case the teasing vision contributed to
his torture. And so from writing like the above he could turn in
the path of a circular psychology from happiness to melancholy;
he could fancy that he was experiencing an accession of the queer
strength which was his between the time of his War Bulletins and
the time he wrote the Booth poem. He could write, "I have to
grow up and be a statesman. I just can't be a boy any longer."

Though he feared New York, though he had been greatly damaged by the iota-subscripts of the reviewing world, he was still
carrying on a correspondence with many of them, as he had done
for years. He was still giving them honorable place in his prefaces,
as he had put them into "The Golden Book of Springfield." One
can't escape the feeling that these were obsequious gestures; they
make a false note in Lindsay's character. He was a good deal of
the time wise as a serpent, but when struck on the head he could
mourn like the dove, and hang the wounded brow and speak soft
words to dissuade enmity from dealing further blows.

His handwriting now showed signs of degenerating. Sometimes he wrote a rolling Spencerian hand which made the page look like a poster; again he wrote with a stub-pen which gave his script the appearance of being done with a Chinese brush. He abandoned his asceticism to the extent of taking up cigarette smoking; he drank coffee to excess; and he changed his mind on Prohibition. "The dry issue is a private and personal question." So Springfield had said to him in the days of the War Bulletins and of his crusades for Prohibition and chastity in the name of Sir Galahad. After countless prayers to Lord Christ, after seeing Christ in a vision as Immanuel playing a harp, he chose Buddha as the chief character of history, and the American flag, not the cross, as the object of his highest devotion.

All the while he was occupied with self-analysis. He was resisting a sort of electrolysis of soul with the immense egoism and pride which he had inherited from the Frasee blood, his mother's people. He was now habitually thinking back to the days of his precocity at six years; and every influence of that far time from his grandfather Frasee demanded that he be restored in these turbulent forties to some Olympian aspect. He was having dizzy spells on the platform, and was in terror lest some time he would collapse before an audience. He thought these attacks were the result of cutting his nerves into three pieces to win first honors in creative work in speaking, writing and drawing; and that he had rhythmic exhaustion.

At the Chicago Art Institute and at Hiram College he went without proper food and had insufficient sleep; and his diaries show a course of reading, and hours of reading which are prodigious, and remind one of the student days of Shelley. He thought that these sedulous, tireless days had damaged his constitution; but something more fundamental was eating away his life than those faraway indiscretions. His mother as a very young woman suffered a severe sunstroke which wrecked her nerves for life. Lindsay was born with a caul over his face which the midwives in the days of Chrysostom sold for magic rites, and as an implement of prophetic power. To come to something more scientifically concrete, mention should be made of the heart attack which he had just before going to Gulfport in 1923; and another which he had shortly after his marriage in 1925.

I first began to know Lindsay while the Spoon River Anthology was in the flush of its acceptance. At that time my visits to Springfield were frequent, as my father and mother lived there. My mother and Lindsay's mother were cordial friends; and on one occasion when I was there Lindsay and I were entertained at dinner at the home of the caretaker of the Lincoln monument, whose wife was a cultivated woman, and a friend of my mother's. Between this time and 1920 I saw Lindsay in Chicago frequently, which in those years was a Mecca for writers from all over the world. I saw him in 1925 when he came to New York with his bride; and again in the Spring of 1926, when he was in New York and had a meal with me at the Players Club. At this last meeting he did not seem greatly changed from the man I knew in Springfield; though upon reflection I know that he was not the rugged man that he seemed. He stood perhaps five feet nine inches, and seemed to weigh from 150 to 160 pounds. His hair was sandy brown, his eyes gray to yellowish-bluish, his nose large and fleshy, his brow retreating, and with a Neandertal ridge over the eyes.

His jaws swept and curved from the ear to the chin, which was rather pointed and stuck forward with assertion. His mouth was ample, with the upper lip protruding beyond the lower. Its gulley from the nose down was deep. When he talked the corners of his mouth clung together, giving at times a sort of lisp to his enunciation. The whole contour of his head was a rhythm which swept back like a leaning zero. He looked at times like Pierrot, like a clown with the paint washed off. This leaning sweep of his head was accentuated by his posture when facing one in conversation. Then it seemed further thrown back, and his eyes squinted elephant-wise, as if he were not sure of the tenor of what was being said to him, whether it was friendly or satirical. These mannerisms had the appearance of vanity and self-sufficiency, and he had both those qualities.

On this occasion I could see that he had been cut into humilities by indifference and ridicule. He said to me that at the beginning of his career he had to bar the door of his hotel in New York, and employ a secretary to answer the telephone, and to turn away interviewers, but now no one noticed him. I told him that this was perfectly natural; that he was no longer a curiosity; that New York had seen and heard him, and had turned to other novelties. But he was not comforted. When we parted I saw he was an unhappy man; and as he walked away from the club I stood and watched him as he went toward Fourth avenue, rolling from side to side like a tired man, and casting up his head as if talking to himself as he proceeded and disappeared. It then occurred to me that he was not the strong man that he seemed to be. From New York he wrote to his wife that he was no longer wanted there, and that people had shown it plainly enough.

Not as Shelley, who thirsted for the "music that is divine," Lindsay according to his nature dreamed of home, of ships of love that would take him thither; hence his wandering from Springfield to Gulfport, and from there to Spokane, and from there back to Springfield was a trail of blood. Everywhere he dwelt in cuckoo cloudland; and it was not wonderful that though he had been driven out of Springfield he could yet dream of that place as an "old battered, scratched violin," where he could recapture his art, and play at last his "most modern and ultra tunes." What he really needed was a vegetable garden, an old house, an old chair, and a contented spirit. He needed to grow up. The curled darling of his mother, the child wonder of the high-school had become a man in body, but with a Narcissism which stunted his development.

It was not out of key that he saw every soul as a circus, and that he could reduce human existence to the tropes of the sawdust ring. Even Jesus, with him, was a sort of Santa Claus. He coupled angels and clowns in his imaginings; Christmas trees abounded everywhere; and when he saw Heaven it was under the white top. When he dreamed of love it was with an equestrienne with whom he would dance and howl for God, while he whirled her over his head, and the two of them leaped from white horses to the rings of Saturn. The imagery of the Old Testament exactly suited a creativeness so evangelical, though in his thinking moments he could speak, as Jefferson did, of the prophetical writings as ravings.

V

Springfield gave Lindsay a welcome, and he settled down in the old house which had been reclaimed for him by a leasehold arrangement. He planned now to force on America a complete new conception of music; a complete new conception of Americanism; a complete set of new religious ideas; a complete set of new ideas of design. He hoped to surpass William Morris as an artist, after a quarter of a century of making drawings which were utterly bad, and after the most friendly critics had told him that he could not draw; and what is more, after repeated confessions to his diary, and even in prefaces, that he had no talent as an artist.

With all this appalling programme on his mind, he started forth
to lecture, to pay taxes on the old house in Springfield, and to
meet the expenses of a growing family, as he now had two children.
Traveling about wearily, he went to places of lost happiness, only
to find the old faces gone, and new faces in their stead to whom
he meant little. Then he would write to his wife, "What I am
really hungry for is my youth that will never return."

At this time he was a young man of fifty, as the virile Franklin
referred to himself at that age. But fatigue had entered Lindsay
so deeply that no sleep but that of death could rest him. The
picture taken of him when he arrived in Springfield in the Spring
of 1929 shows the face of a man smoothed round by soft middle-
age fat. Senility had already taken him, and he knew it. Like
Grover Cleveland he was mortified by the youth of his wife, and
what he felt was the unfitting age of himself. No torture of the
mind was spared him. He began to say that the whole world was
his enemy and was in a conspiracy against him; and he had as
much ground for believing this as Shelley had, or Dante.

In the Summer of 1931 he rested near Hazelhurst, Wis., where
he sojourned incognito. "My head is clear as a bell for reading,"
he wrote to his wife. "It's my poor heart that needs the harness.
There is no vacation for my heart. Always it will tear itself cruelly
for you. And 1 know you need kindness and wise coöperation from
me. Desperate love does not help." He asked her to practice the
piano so that she could play for him during the ensuing Winter.
By that music he hoped to drive the "clickety Pullmans and the
jazz" from his heart; he hoped for sleep that bromides and luminal
would not produce. His letters of these days are autumnal wails;
they are gray with the mists of a dying soul.

He would have been better off as a celibate; but after forty he
could not stand the loneliness. At the time he married he had
reached the point where some sort of companionship and satisfaction of desire had become imperative. But the discipline of
marriage killed the mystic in him; and this was more nails in his
feet. What he really wanted was union with the god-head, and
next to that was his dream of America. Any other form of marriage
was really an impertinence, a sacrilege, an impossibility, and a
source of disillusionment, conflict, pain, disaster and death.

When he saw this in moments made clairvoyant by his suffering,
he considered wandering off to Hiram College, there to read and
write, as he had done as a youth of eighteen. Again he contem-

plated taking to the road and beggary again. Life had caught him, and he did not know which way to turn, or what to do. His attitude toward sex was complicated by a poor sex education, by his fear and hatred, love and dependence upon his mother, by a morbid fear of old age and frantic hunger for youth, by waiting too long for a normal sex life, by the unhappiness of his own parents together, by a Tolstoyian conviction that sex was debasing, by his aversion to reality, by the tragical loneliness which is always the concomitant of genius. Added to all this was a pronounced case of virgin fixation, of mariolatry, of which his letters to his wife are full, telling her of dreams that he had of the Virgin Mary, and asking her somehow to have the same dreams.

The time was come, too, when every injury done him came back into his mind fresh as on the day of its infliction, and even redoubled in its malignancy. Among all the persons who had hurt him he saw his mother as one of the chief. When his sister asked him to dedicate a book to her memory he wrote to his wife that he was expected to do it "in spite of the fact that my mother fought me like a wild cat over every poem I wrote till she found Oxford listening to me. My mother had great qualities, and I tried to do them justice in 'Adventures While Singing These Songs,' which covered the ground till I was seven or eight; but whatever I owe my mother or father, I certainly do not owe them the dedication of a single line I ever wrote. 'The Hearth Eternal' is an idealized picture of her."

On the other hand, in moments of soundest judgment, Lindsay esteemed his father, and longed for that "Old Cinnamon Bear," to clothe his son with the virility and common sense which distinguished him. Many books have been written to show that Christianity has emasculated the world, that it shoved aside the enlightenment and the wisdom of Hellas for a doctrine of superstition and ignorance and weakness, and thereby put the control of the world into the hands of the dregs and the unwashed and the Gadarenes, led by clerics, bigots and demagogues; and that it supplanted the rich, profound and life-giving Plato by the epileptic Saint Paul. Lindsay's life and work are other instances of what Christianity can do to a mind. In Greece he would have sat at the feet of Pindar and Theocritus.

In spite of his ultimate opinion of his mother he carried to the day of his death a sheet of paper on which she had written Browning's lines:

Grow old along with me
The best is yet to be,
The last of life for which the first was made.

He tried with all his might to believe that the best was yet to
be. But neither a moral will long exercised, a really heroic mastery
at times of congenital weaknesses, nor religious faith, nor love of
Christ, could save him from the blackness of despair which settled
clear to the horizon in the Fall of 1931. In judging of his career,
even in adequately appraising what he wrote, full consideration
must be given to the handicaps he overcame, to the defective
mentality which he corrected in a measure, to his resolution, to
his will to see life as good and as happiness, to the songs of joy
that he sang in spite of pain and ridicule and discouragement. His
life so regarded was a radiant triumph of morality over great
obstacles. For at last, although he wrote pages of sorry trash, his
best work constitutes the largest body of inspired lyricism which
any American has contributed to literature. He had more ideas
than Poe, and nobler and saner ideas; and by that test "The
Chinese Nightingale," "The John Brown Trilogy," "Old, Old, Old,
Old Andrew Jackson" and "The Virginians Are Coming Again,"
are greater poems than "The Raven" or "Ulalume." What in
Coleridge is so original as these poems of Lindsay's?

VI

On November 30 he gave a lecture at the First Christian Church
of Springfield. He had returned from a tour in the late Fall, which
was marked by a distressing discourtesy in Washington. For some
reason the audience there, to the extent of about two hundred
persons, walked from the auditorium. With all that has been re-
counted, this Washington humiliation was deep in Lindsay's mor-
tification; and in the week before his death he showed alarming
symptoms, though a slight diabetes and a somewhat high blood
pressure seemed satisfactorily corrected. The Springfield appearance was a heartening experience. When he found the audience
large and cordial, and the applause enthusiastic as he ended, he
turned to a friend, saying, "I feel that at last I have won Springfield."

But this success contained no heart cure of moment. The week
following he was up and down in bed, at times too exhausted to
go about safely. The afternoon before his death he was at a tea
with his wife, where his laughter and humor seemed assuring on

the matter of his peace of mind, his ultimate restoration to health. But these were merely surface phenomena of really ominous import, if they had been rightly diagnosed. They were the smiles of a man taking possession of all his stored-up heroism to face the end. That night at home he became very weak and fatigued, his wife finding him in bed before the dinner hour when she returned from an errand. He came down to dinner, but ate little, and wept as he said that he was an old man, and that his career was ended. He returned to bed, but could not stay there; and so he was in bed and out of bed wandering about the house, descending and ascending the stairs, going over his books, and the photographs of his wife and children. At last his wife, who had fallen asleep for a few minutes toward 12:30, was awakened and in the morning heard him about the house, and went to the hallway in time to see him fall by the door of his room. He was put in bed, but died before a physician could arrive, who assigned as the cause of death the clogging of the coronary artery.

His funeral was as distinguished as sorrow could make it, and the desire to erase past neglect could contrive. The City Council of Springfield and the Legislature of Illinois passed resolutions of respect, and sermons and orations filled Springfield at the churches and in the schools, to the accompaniment of many tributes from the American press far and near. He was buried not far from the tomb of Lincoln, and committed to the centuries as his idol had been sixty-seven years before.

> The much deceived Endymion
> Slips behind a tomb.

W. R. Moses

Vachel Lindsay: Ferment of the Poet's Mind

The nearer ancestors of Vachel Lindsay were characterized by a considerable number of interests and perhaps talents. Lindsay's father, a country doctor, a Kentuckian by birth and blood, never forgave Lincoln for the Civil War. He was a fanatical prohibitionist, moreover, and a hater of tobacco. Lindsay's mother's father was a farmer and a Campbellite preacher, a sympathizer with the Northern cause although he had brothers who fought for the South, and an enthusiast in cattle breeding. Lindsay's mother was a clever woman, whose intellectual activity was directed by the early training she received in a strict Campbellite household. She liked painting, and before her marriage taught art in two small mid-western colleges. After marriage her activity was polyphase: she wrote strange playlets with a religious or moral cast, wrote and delivered speeches, especially on art, organized societies, visited Europe, urged civic reform, read religious books, studied works on Egypt and Confucius, stood strong for Americanism, believed in and tried to spread her belief in social perfectibility, fought the

From *Southern Review*, I (September 1936), 828-36. Reprinted by permission of Louisiana State University Press.

saloon and the diversions of the idle and godless of Springfield, opposed corruption in government, and strove for a democracy in which God's laws should prevail and men be equal as high-minded and devout citizens. I feel grateful to Edgar Lee Masters* for presenting these facts, and believe that he is correct in his observation that Lindsay's intellectual heritage from his mother included various conflicts which the poet was never able to straighten out.

The Mason-Dixon line ran straight through his heart, Lindsay said. His parentage made that very natural. More importantly and more unfortunately, he inherited an inclination to save the world as well as to paint and to write, and a tendency to unite the reforming urge with the artistic urge arbitrarily, if he could not do it otherwise. The enthusiasms of his parents had a counterpart, if not a result, in manifold longings and activities that characterized their son from his early youth uninterruptedly until his death. Very commendably, Masters has included in his biography such voluminous quotations from Lindsay's early diaries that the ferment of the poet's mind is wide open to observation.

At Hiram College, where he studied medicine ostensibly and poetry and oratory really, Lindsay at one time kept six notebooks. Each contains the dedication, "This book belongs to Christ," though the subjects of the six were, respectively, study of the dictionary, rhetoric, phrases, verses, new words, "when nothing else"; culture; homiletics; style; speaking; and pictures. The entries are the records of introspective examinings, plans for conduct and attainment, speculations—often dogmatic and often fatuous —as to the truth of things. Moral and religious reflections are extremely numerous. In the notebook on rhetoric, for example, this kind of thing is early included: "In the world there are two forces, nature which extends through every function of man, and love whereby man may be divine in power. Two beings, God and man. No commands of Christ are impossible. Follow every commandment vigorously. Get even with the devil. Comply with the conditions by which Christ keeps possession of men . . ." Not only during his college period but for long afterwards, Lindsay was deeply obsessed with religion and Christ, a secular Christ who should serve as practical leader and example in the modern world. All his life Lindsay remained true to Campbellite theology; more or less guided by it he drew his specifications for his "Map of the Universe." Also, that theology is not quite lost sight of in *The*

---

* *Vachel Lindsay: A Poet in America.* New York: Scribner's.

Golden Book of Springfield, a vague and unimpressive work in which the nebulous mysticism attracts less attention than the damp sentimentality with which the author depicts conflict between beautiful righteous people and ugly wicked ones in his Springfield of the future after it is, presumably at least, well on the way towards the ideal. But something was wrong with either Lindsay or his religion, for the latter failed to stand by its possessor in a serious pinch, and never determined a definite code for him or for other people. Masters evaluates it thus: "It was superstition as a plaything, a spectacle that always engrossed Lindsay's imagination. It was a show, a circus. His Christ was out of Santa Claus, his paradise out of the baubles of Christmas." I am afraid the evaluation is correct.

Some of the poet's other tastes and activities were to a degree connected with his religion. For example, there was the admiration of the Y. M. C. A. which he recorded in his Hiram notebooks. There was also his lengthy period of lecturing on art under Y. M. C. A. auspices; and doubtless his verbal campaigning in behalf of the Anti-Saloon League as well.

At the same time, he had a quantity of interests not necessarily dependent on, or connected with, religion. In college days and for years afterwards he studied art assiduously, although he never became able to draw well, remained all his life largely engrossed with the trivial and fanciful as subject matter, and for long held the notion that his studies were chiefly directed to the end of his becoming a Christian cartoonist. When about twenty he made elaborate plans for preparation for world-saving, plans involving more or less extended periods of residence in, and thorough mastery of the spirits of, Chicago, France, and Japan. He loved hieroglyphics, or the idea of hieroglyphics—symbols to fix the reality, the soul, of his country. And he loved his country deeply, in many aspects. Perhaps his Middle-West, soil and people and traditions, was deepest in his affections, yet at times he described himself as a Kentuckian by accident born in Illinois; again he loved Virginia above other sections; and late in life he had fine (though also harsh) words for the west coast. He liked Kansas, too—it all went into the melting pot to produce the "soul of the U. S. A.," which was his quest (though in one poem he proposed allying himself with gipsies and returning with them, in the distant future to India). He lauded men he took to represent the best Americanism—Johnny Appleseed, Jefferson, Jackson, Lincoln, and such. He idealized the log cabin as an American symbol. But he also praised the motion picture, and certain other aspects of modernity. He went afield in time and space, developed enthusiasms for Egypt and China. He was never free from the turmoil of his imagination, and the manifold conceptions, too many of them tinselly affairs, it produced.

Certainly I have not adequately represented the extent or yet the confusion of Lindsay's interests. Yet many as they were, few of the interests seemed to receive adequate representation in Lindsay's poetry. A soft nature to begin with, the poet could rarely see reality clearly and penetratingly, and from his inability, triviality frequently resulted. I suggest that Campbellite theology may very possibly have furnished him with an excuse, perhaps without his being conscious of what was happening, for regarding the next world as more important than this one. Thus it may have been easy for him to devote too much of his attention to vague jungles of heaven or palaces of Eve on the one hand, and to circuses, insects, and fairies on the other, instead of to efforts to attain the clear vision the poet seems to need.

Anyhow, Lindsay very early began writing, often to illustrate drawings in the same mood, verses about insects, fairies, moons, and their like. I do not know the date of the composition of "The Tree of Laughing Bells," but the date is unimportant, for Lindsay's manner of writing never changed significantly. The poem begins thus:

> From many morning-glories
> That in an hour will fade,
> From many pansy buds
> Gathered in the shade,
> From lily of the valley
> And dandelion buds,
> And fiery poppy buds
> Are the Wings of Morning made

The triviality and lack of distinction here must be evident immediately; and often Lindsay wrote more crudely, occasionally more childishly. At best his moon and insect and similar poems are no more than sprightly. As he wrote such poems early, so he wrote them late; his last volume, *Every Soul Is a Circus*, is chiefly composed of them.

True, in the latter part of his life especially, Lindsay claimed to be writing much of his poetry to be danced, not read. High school freshmen, apparently, did most of the dancing. Let it suffice to remark that the poet seemingly did not do enough in the theory and practice of dance-poetry to establish the canon of a new art, and that according to present standards you cannot justify, or rather make important, trivial poetry by saying you meant it as a substitute for dance-music.

Thus a good-sized portion of Lindsay's poetry may be, for most purposes, dismissed. I have already suggested a possible reason for the poet's too-great concern with, and yet careless treatment of, the unimportant. But frequently he wrote seriously and intellectually of the important—American heroes, or the majestic Springfield to be. When he wrote in that manner of the important, unfortunately, he had a tendency to put together vague and threadbare phraseology in haphazard iambic pentameter—by "haphazard" iambic pentameter I mean rather sprawling lines in which too often, apparently only through the writer's carelessness, the heavy beats come on *and's, the's,* and *of's.*

The very well known "Abraham Lincoln Walks at Midnight" is a satisfactory example of another type of defect. The sixth stanza is:

> The sins of all the war-lords burn in his heart.
> He sees the dreadnaughts scouring every main.
> He carries on his shawl-wrapped shoulders now
> The bitterness, the folly and the pain.

I cannot be much pleased by a figure as crude and also vague as that in the first line; nor be quite satisfied with the indefinite description of Lincoln's Atlas-burden. Vagueness is the fault, too, of Lindsay's conception of the Springfield or the Middle-West of the future, and of his writings about city or region. Springfield was to become the place of love and joy and art and beauty and great men, but, apart from a very few such qualifications as small size, one has nothing definite to guide him in imagining the splendid city-to-be. His imagination cannot take hold of it; therefore he cannot to the highest degree be satisfied with it. A reader would hardly demand that poems about the city contain complete verbal blueprints for it, but he might legitimately ask to be spared the mist hanging about joy, love, and beauty. *The Golden Book of Springfield* (to attempt to compare which with *The Republic* would be ridiculous) ought to contain something in the nature of verbal blueprints.

Lindsay wrote a great deal of miscellaneous poetry, but having criticized the moon-poem group and the serious discussions I feel that I may proceed to a mention of the group which nearly everybody believes to be Lindsay's best. It can be observed incidentally that most of the miscellaneous poetry is characterized by some degree of vagueness or triviality or both.

Masters lists the "best" poems, and his listing is satisfactory for present purposes, as "The Chinese Nightingale," "In Praise of Johnny Appleseed," "The Santa Fe Trail," "The Booker Washington Trilogy," "The Congo," "Poems Speaking of Buddha, Prince Siddartha," "Old, Old, Old, Old Andrew Jackson," "The Virginians Are Coming Again," and "Bryan, Bryan, Bryan, Bryan." I do not wish to discuss these individually at very great length. All are vigorous, all redundant, all or nearly all graced by memorable lines, and all injured by the fact, mentioned more than once by Masters, that Lindsay saw everything through his peculiar colored glasses. I am neither ignorant of nor quarrelsomely inclined towards the truism that every poet sees things individually; I believe only that Lindsay's personal vision was in general unimpressive, partly through allegiance to unsatisfactory mythology and partly through simple blindness to matter of fact. I shall mention this matter further, and likewise the fact that the poet's system of beliefs—naturally anyone's system of beliefs determines how he sees the world—never saw harmony established between its constituent elements. "The Chinese Nightingale," now, written chiefly in the headlong iambic with sprinkled anapests and more or less irregular line-length and rhyme scheme that seem to distinguish all of Lindsay's "best" poems, depends pretty largely, like all the "best" poems, upon its vigor, without which it would appear sprawling and sentimental. Sentimental to a degree it is anyhow, but not troublesomely so, on the contrary characterized by a good deal of what seems genuine sentiment. The familiar line, "Spring came on forever," is broadly appealing. Let me remark, however, that it is hard to believe the poem has anything peculiarly Chinese about it except a little external paraphernalia. It seems the result of an interest used because of the romantic flavor that could be infused into it by the poet without really mastering it. "In Praise of Johnny Appleseed" suffers from two things notably: an inadequacy of conception of the nature of the early westward migrations that makes the beginning of the poem, with its ideal symbolization of that movement, unduly high-flown to say the least of it; and the already mentioned vagueness of conception of the splendid America to come that makes the latter part of the poem unsatisfactory. (With Lindsay subject matter was so frankly placed before form that one need make no bones of objecting to subject matter as such; and although inadequate conception of subject matter may not injure a poem's first impact, it unquestionably does injure its power of satisfying permanently.) "The Santa Fe Trail," again, is vigorous and indefinite, but a sound enough juxtaposition of the blatancy of mechanical progress and principles of beauty—however mistily expressed—not to be overcome by the blatancy.

The first poem of "The Booker Washington Trilogy," "Simon Legree," stands pretty well by itself, an arresting fancy adequately expressed in what Masters may be correct in regarding as transmuted hymn rhythms. The second, "John Brown," may be questioned on the same grounds as the first part of "In Praise of Johnny Appleseed"—questionably proper conception of the subject. The third, a "poem game" entitled "King Solomon and the Queen of Sheba," seems somewhat thin for its length, and indicates rather its author's liking for the spectacular than anything else. Lindsay's familiar "boom" poem, "The Congo," impresses me as very much more satisfactory in its first section, with its terrific symbolization of cannibal savagery, than in the later sections, where the Congo cannibals are gratuitously brought to a Christian heaven at last. One cannot but sympathize with poor Lindsay, by the way, in his impatience with the conception of him as a rackety jazz poet which audiences persisted in holding, thanks mostly to "The Congo" and "General William Booth Enters Heaven." I object to the two short units of "Poems Speaking of Buddha, Prince Siddartha," on the ground already given for objecting to such poems as "Abraham Lincoln Walks at Midnight"; and I am out of sympathy, moreover, with addressing Buddha with as much clanging and booming as Lindsay inserts into the longest of this group. The last three poems in Masters' list, "Old, Old, Old, Old Andrew Jackson," "The Virginians Are Coming Again," and "Bryan, Bryan, Bryan, Bryan" may be considered as a group. They are somewhat deeply moving poems, all of them, inspired by noble feelings which show through and inspire parallel feelings in the reader. The power of moving deeply is a valuable asset for a poem. But of these three one might very justifiably complain in the spirit of George Moore objecting to the manifold poems about liberty, equality, and fraternity—not that I should insist at all upon pure poetry, but that just where one takes the loftiest moral ideas as subject matter he should most of all be hard and definite, whereas these poems by Lindsay are not at all hard and definite.

"Not at all hard and definite" would be a satisfactory phrase on which to center my general objections to Lindsay's poetry. That his better poems are to greater or less degree impressive in various respects I have no wish to deny. But it seems that in reading even the best of them one cannot avoid feeling a little uncertain where he is. What is the core of this poetry? I have rehearsed a list of Lindsay's main beliefs or enthusiasms. A number of them are visible in the "best" poems just mentioned, and although one were to insert other poems for some of those of Masters' preference, the essential heterogeneity of the group as it now stands would not probably be simplified. How does one establish working unity between love of romantic China, of Buddha, of negro characteristics and attitudes, of Old Testament theology, and of the best features of the American spirit, as exemplified in great Americans, to say nothing of love of these things and of the various other things that drew Lindsay's affections? The poet under discussion certainly did not answer the question, or show other people how to answer it.

The result of his failure need not have been, and indeed was not, inability to produce good individual poems. It was, in the personal field, probably at least a contributory cause to the unhappiness of the poet's last years and death. In the field of poetry it was failure to produce a sufficient body of work directed to one definite end to give the impressive effect of mass, something to be guided by or to contemplate with intellectual satisfaction, that we usually perceive in the work of great poets; that we gain from, indeed, Lindsay's biographer's own Spoon River Books. I know—I have said a number of times—that Lindsay was devoted to the idea of a great America and a great Springfield, but—I have also said several times—he did not clearly enough define the objects of his devotion to make his celebrations of them thoroughly satisfying. The poet's intellectual inheritance, it would seem, played him false through its very profusion. That Lindsay was impelled, through his heritage or otherwise, to reform the world was probably unfortunate, though not in that it made his poetry propagandistic. It does not seem to be of moment whether poetry is propagandistic or not; the trouble is that the writer urged by too great love of reform is likely to concentrate on the *what* and neglect the *how*, to the eternal detriment of both *what* and *how*. Lindsay wrote too vaguely, and in general too carelessly otherwise.

Thus it seems proper to conclude that among the plethora of his interests Lindsay's mind did not so much grow as ferment, and that his greatest defect was the familiar one of failure to establish a really satisfactory point of view. For this reason and for his congenital inability to see things as they are—an inability Masters stresses without, it seems to me, deducing all he should from it— Lindsay cannot without question be termed the spokesman of America, though close enough analogy may exist between his confusion and that of America in general. I should not for a moment question his sincerity and the worthiness of his purpose, or his historical importance (though I have had no reason to speak of that); but I feel that in declaring the listed "best" poems, with a further list of "second best" poems, to constitute the most considerable body of imaginative lyricism that any American has produced, Masters somewhat overstates Lindsay's greatness.

Austin Warren

The Case of Vachel Lindsay

Nothing that Lindsay did came off triumphantly. He couldn't be treated like Emerson in Arnold's famous essay: not this, not this, not this, but that. Lindsay's story, narrated by Edgar Lee Masters, is sad, grotesque, instructive. The book belongs with Horton's *Hart Crane*, Foster Damon's *Amy Lowell*, and Hagedorn's *Robinson*—all honest, painful chronicles of "what it means to be a poet in the U.S."

Vachel Lindsay was not only an American, but a Middle Westerner, and very conscious of it—or, conscious, at least, of not being an Easterner. For him, America divided into the wealthy, genteel, intellectual Eastern seaboard (the hated, supercilious New England) and the rest of the country.

A proud citizen of Springfield, Illinois, he felt early hostility to the bearded Massachusetts poets whose pictures appeared in the literature textbooks and whose claims to represent "culture" were asserted by the schoolmarm. His heroes were the extra-canonical Poe and Whitman, and later Mark Twain (whose *Huck Finn* he quite modernly saw.)

From *Accent,* VI (Summer 1946), 230-39. Reprinted by permission of *Accent* and the author.

Lindsay's stock on both sides were solid, middle-class Protestants. Grandpa Lindsay, of Gallatin County, Kentucky, died "unreconstructed." Grandpa Frazee, of Indiana, was a farmer, a breeder of cattle and horses, a lay preacher. Vachel's father, "Dr. Mohawk," was a country doctor who travelled around in an old buggy stuffed with bottles and surgical instruments. Otherwise to name him, he was a fanatical prohibitionist and anti-nicotinist, vigorously masculine and black-bearded, proud of having worked his way to independence and respected position.

Vachel was a golden-curled "mother's boy": he loved and hated his mother, found her absurd and domineering, pathetic, massive, and necessary. In Mary Baker Eddy (as portrayed by Ida Tarbell) Lindsay found "the same kind of person, who requires enormous long-range activities to keep from overmanaging all those nearby." Lindsay was over forty when she died; the year following, he suffered a nervous breakdown from which he never completely recovered:—

Lindsay's "case" is his great interest. Why didn't he come off as a poet? Probably the best answer is: he was "torn between" too many opposing forces, forces which he couldn't really comprehend, couldn't properly name, let alone resolve.

He was neither a completely "uneducated poet," or autodidact, nor yet a "civilized" poet: he venerated museums of historic art, while, on the other hand, sponsoring the idea of a "popular" and *lively* art . . . His best bet certainly lay in the latter. The "cultivated" side of Lindsay is largely "sissy" and vapid. He hadn't mind enough or taste enough to take the line of Stevens or Eliot. Meanwhile, though he kept protesting that he was not a "jazz" poet—that he hated jazz, he certainly liked its religious equivalent in the gospel hymns, and as certainly wanted to create a lowbrow art. Certainly he envied the vitality of the lowbrows, the vitality of "Dionysiac" religion.

There is another confusion in Lindsay,—of regionalism and internationalism. Each nation has its own culture: quite rightly he hated the condescension with which 100% Americans treated "newcomers"—"new Americans" (dagoes, sheenies, etc.); remembered that Italy had produced Dante and da Vinci as well as the banana vendor. So Lindsay hated New England condescension to South and Middle West, and American condescension to foreigners —wanted a regional culture.

This strain in Lindsay might have led him to a kind of Middle Western Fascism. It prompted him to attack the East coast and

Europe as effete, and to prefer Evangelical, Fundamentalist, revivalist Protestantism, which would be, of course, an agrarian and Jeffersonian Protestantism—like that of Grandpa Frazee. Out of this self Lindsay can write (to Professor Armstrong, of Baylor Baptist University, Texas):

> The coeducational, Middle West denominational college is to me the highest point in American civilization . . . I believe profoundly in our agricultural and Middle West civilization and think it the natural America. . . . I greatly mistrust industrial America, radical or conservative . . . I want in some sense to represent the honest, clean, devout young Americans who are courting and studying Browning and saying their prayers on campuses like yours. I disagree with them a great deal, but . . . I am more keenly aware of how I differ from everything east of the Mississippi River or Springfield, in Europe or America.

But this strain is countered by another,—an eclectic and liberal religiosity. Just as his mother's "great achievement" was uniting all the women's missionary societies of Springfield, Illinois, so in Vachel there was a good deal of the "reunionizer" of "the churches"—"There's good in *all* the churches." Lindsay didn't permanently remain a Fundamentalist Evangelical, however much he liked that mask; after his teens he is best, if untechnically, described as a "theosophist" or "esoteric Christian." Like Yeats, Babbitt, and Huxley, he believed that we could learn from the Wisdom of the East as well as from Occidental Christianity. As for Christianity, he was Catholic as well as Campbellite, and Swedenborgian into the bargain. There is a kind of common denominator in Lindsay's religiosity: it is never theological, but unites the Dionysiac ("mystical" he would have called it) with the humanitarian (thought of generally in an Apocalyptic light.) Such eclecticism prompted Lindsay's dream of a cathedral for his home town, one which should have altars to all reputable gods and heroes. He hoped for a creedless religion, shared by all kind and art-loving people.

Analogous was his dream of a synoptic American culture to which the Irish, the Jew, the Pole, and the Negro should each make his own distinctive contribution. Lindsay's Y. M. C. A. art class in New York was composed of policemen, street-car conductors—Italians, Greeks, Jews. He printed off some of his poems and at nights went in shops along Tenth Avenue selling them—visited Chinese laundries; listened to the street services of the Salvation

Army. These were not Lindsay's stock: he was partly a Quixote, partly a cultural missionary. But he also had his silent, unnamed community with the despised and the rejected—the wop and the sheeny and the chink, for Lindsay himself was an involuntary "outsider." Like E. A. Robinson, he longed for the admiration of the solid, Anglo-Saxon, Protestant citizens of his home town. Both would have coveted Emerson's happy fortune of being respected by Concord as well as celebrated by the intelligentsia; but at that ambition neither succeeded. Lindsay was the Bronson Alcott of Springfield. He had the backing of the local "liberals," had his own little circle, composed of Single Taxers, Swedenborgians, and high school teachers. But that didn't really satisfy him, for he didn't command the world of his mother and father: they and their kind didn't take him seriously.

In 1926 Lindsay entrusted to the *Saturday Evening Post* a painful, eloquent confession of "What It Means to be a Poet in America." Reared on the Romantic poets and the Romantic conception of Milton, Lindsay thought of the poet as *vates*. "Poets are the unacknowledged legislators of the nations." His view of the poet as myth-maker instead of verse-writer led him to the thesis that before the Civil War our real poets were our statesmen —Jefferson, Hamilton, Lincoln.

The poet as imaginative statesman passes into the poet as saint and martyr. Lindsay early identified himself with the Messiah: thought of himself as, till thirty, preparing for his ministry, spoke of the crucifixion of the Middle West artist, dreamed of crucified angels and thorny crowns. About the later Lindsay there was, according to Masters, much of the bishop—something sacerdotal and pontifical. On his walking trips of 1908 and 1912, he was also, of course, a friar, a mendicant, clad in the garb of poverty and chastity, going forth to preach the Gospel of Beauty. A Franciscan, he was also an itinerant Protestant, like Johnny Appleseed: he scattered his poems as Johnny scattered his leaves from Swedenborg.

Lindsay never subscribed to the "didactic heresy" nor to the Orphic. He is a propagandist, but not in verse; and he is never an intellectual poet. The chief Lindsay poems—public pieces for oral performance—might be genealogically understood in terms of "The Bells" and "The Raven," "When Lilacs Last," and "O, Pioneers." Poe is suggested by Lindsay's fondness for onomatopoeic effects and the more obvious phonetic devices (strongly marked rhythms, plentiful rhyme, alliteration); Whitman, by the search for an American myth, a democratic tradition made imaginative.

"The priest departs; the divine literatus comes." *Democratic Vistas* bespeaks the need of a new democratic poetry, to succeed that of feudalism. Lindsay's chief response is by creating an American mythology—this is partly a series of folk-heroes (folk-versions of folk-heroes)—Andrew Jackson, William Jennings Bryan, Johnny Appleseed, Alexander Campbell, and General William Booth, partly through mythic poems. These hero-pieces attempt to make a popular regional poetry—legends, so to speak. Two other chief Lindsay poems—"The Chinese Nightingale" and "The Congo"—grow out of Lindsay's "home missionary" spirit.

2

Lindsay was slow in finding focus. He had passed thirty when his "General Booth" was published, when his first book (of which that is the titular poem) was lauded by Howells, Masefield, Chesterton, and then the generality. From 1913 until his suicide in 1931, he was a public figure, making tours of the states as a "reader"—a chanter or rhapsode of his own works.

He developed considerable shrewdness in the course of these tours. The letters to one of his managers, Professor Armstrong, might be those of a Protestant revivalist or of a political candidate like his admired Bryan. He is selling poetry to the nation. He goes to work organizing the campaign—passing good-humored judgment on rival organizers and promoters like Amy Lowell, Harriet Monroe, and the *London Mercury's* J. C. Squire. He thinks of himself as a pioneer and road-breaker; recommends Robinson, Frost, and Percy Mackaye to "follow up" with more considered and intensive work. A proper son of his mother, he thinks of such a nation-wide campaign as carried on through existing organizations. He does not, however, use the Chautauqua circuits; nor will he use the women's clubs, which, he writes Professor Armstrong, "are for the most part made up of rich, middle-aged women that their husbands put on a salary to let them alone." His chosen instrumentality is to be another peculiarly American institution— the "English department," in both high schools and colleges the purveyor of general culture, from radical ideology to theatre and music; and his local agent, everywhere, is to be that "local versifier and troubadour who is disguised as an English instructor."

"English departments," in contrast to the women's clubs, were moulders of young, still educable Americans. But Lindsay's evangelical ambition was not satiate when he had taught the teachers. He thirsted to reach and "influence" the American males who guided the opinions of other adult males. In his successful days, he noted bitterly that the local newspaper editor, the "owner of the mind of the town," never attended the dinners given in his honor. If he was constantly, in those same years, invited to appear before the Rotary, the Kiwanis, the Lions, and the Optimists, composed of the leading business and professional men of Middletown, he was not fooled: they expected him to *amuse* them, to "do his stuff" as a queer new kind of vaudevillian—he who had, he believed, as much to say to the American people as Hoover, Hughes, or Bryan.

What Lindsay offered his evening audiences happily remains to be heard on a series of recordings which includes three of the best poems (as well as the chief show-pieces of his tours,—pieces which, in consequence, he came to detest performing)—"General Booth," "The Congo," "The Chinese Nightingale."*

Lindsay was generally advertised as a "jazz poet," a label he hated. What he patently had in mind to do was, on the one hand, to revive the tradition of oral poetry and the craft of that professional performer called the rhapsode; and, on the other, to ally poetry with the 'lively arts,' to show the American male that poetry needn't be hortatory, hermetic, or otherwise pretentious and boring. Lindsay wanted to unite folk-art with high-brow art. In 1912 he diarized: "Write poems to conform to popular tunes in the outline of their melody, like 'A hot time,' 'After the ball' . . . There ought to be poems on astrology, palmistry . . ." He doesn't mention the Gospel hymns, so-called (by whom first I don't know); but they deserve prominent position in any repertory of American folk-music—these Protestant songs, usually originating in large-scale revivals like those of Moody and Sankey or Billy Sunday and Homer Rodeheaver, which, collected into the "red book" or the "green book," furnish the Dionysiac quality to the "evening preaching service," the "prayer meeting," and the "young people's society." They fall into pretty straightforward categories: primarily the sentimental ("Almost Persuaded,") and the hearty ("Bringing in the Sheaves"). Despite the aversion of older Evangelicals to dancing, the Gospel tunes are heartily rhythmic, in the

---

* The Lindsay disks, originally recorded for William Cabell Greet, are now in the excellent Contemporary Poets' Series of the National Council of Teachers of English.

pattern of the march, the two-step, the polka, the waltz. Lindsay's "Booth" offers as its musical signature one of these rousing hymns particularly suited to performance by Salvation Army bands as well as by pastors, white and black, beating out the accents on the pulpit Bible: "Power, Power, Wonder-working Power in the Precious Blood of the Lamb."

Of course the ancestry of "Booth" and the "Congo" is not so simple as this. It is, clearly, chant-poetry (in contrast to speech-poetry) at which Lindsay aimed. While writing to a musical tune, as Burns and Moore did, gives one song-poetry, chant-poetry is written to a primitive rhythmical pattern such as can be sung-and-danced, or clapped out (as children do their sidewalk games.) The prosodic lineage of the Lindsay poems goes back to the nursery rhymes and specifically to the "dipodic movement" which begins with Kipling's *Barrack-Room Ballads* and is represented in English poetry before 1920 by Noyes, Masefield, and Chesterton. The story of this movement remains to be told, and not all the sequences are yet clear; but there are marked generic denominators: all these poets, from Kipling to Lindsay, are, in reaction against esoteric and subjective poetry, writing popular, balladic oral pieces, generally narrative, rhythmic, aimed at oral performance. This crudely popular poetry is accentual, not syllabic, in its base; and, wherever prose accent and verse accent conflict, it is the tune-pattern which imposes itself, a pattern easily to be got from the lines in which the accents coincide. The basic dipodic rhythm (/ ∪ // ∪) is often a continuum upon which is imposed a more obvious pattern of clustered stresses regularly recurring.

In Masefield, there are the recurrent two-stress clusters ("it's a warm wind, the west wind" or "And the wheel's kick and the wind's song") but there are, though less characteristic, the three-stress clusters, used as cadence (the verse I just cited ends "and the white sail's shaking"; in "Cargoes" the pattern is obvious in the monosyllabic cadences of "sweet white wine" and "cheap tin trays.") Chesterton's "Lepanto" offers, however, the closest parallel to Lindsay's rhythmic "signature," the

("Booth led boldly with his big bass drum'):

Chesterton writes

>   "Strong gongs groaning as the guns boom far,"
>   and
>   "Stiff flags straining in the night-blasts cold."*

Priority is not easy to assign. Untermeyer (*Modern British Poetry*, 233) speaks of "Lepanto" as "anticipating the clanging verses of 'The Congo' "; but "Lepanto" (1915) is antedated by Lindsay's "Booth" (1913) and "Congo" (1914). Masefield and Chesterton gave to Lindsay's *Booth and Other Poems* praise which was recognition of a shared cause.

It is not clear just when Lindsay evolved his special mode of oral performance. His poems require such performance, are not to be judged from an eye-reading of the scores, though one should have the text by him while he listens to Lindsay, who indeed expected his audiences to look and listen at the same time. All poets, even those whose self-consciousness renders them incompetent, are upon occasion invited to give public readings from their work. Lindsay, who, like Cummings, Joyce, and MacLeish, was a brilliant *diseur* as well as poet, must gradually have learned how to implement vocally the phonetic qualities (of rhythm, pitch, timbre, volume) which presumably were in part present to his mind as he originally composed the texts.

Lindsay invoked, as honorific precedent, the union, in the ancient Greek theatre, of dance, song, and literature; but the in-

---

* How to bar off Lindsay's rhythmic signature seems relatively unimportant, though it seems irrelevantly "classical" to speak, as Masters does, of the first foot as a *molossus* (the Greek term for a foot of three long syllables) . . . in which case we must scan the rest of the line as composed of a pyrrhic foot and another molossus. Using the conception of the monosyllabic foot, we can scan: / ′ / ′ / ′ ∪ ∪ ∪ / ′ / ′ / ′ / ;
or, carrying out the dipodic pattern more literally, we can read:

/ Bóoth léd / bóldly with hís / bíg báss / drúm /

The best historical treatment of dipodic and allied meters is in George R. Stewart's *Modern Metrical Technique, as Illustrated by Ballad Meters, 1700-1920* (N. Y., 1922.) On the modern "dipodists" there are excellent remarks in H. W. Wells' *New Poets from Old*. And for a convincing argument that Hopkins' "Sprung rhythm" aimed at another kind of dipody, there is Harold Whitehall's essay in the New Directions *G. M. Hopkins*.

gredients of his own technic can be actually assembled out of more or less traditional forms with which he was familiar: oratory, political and ecclesiastical: the "silver-tongued" eloquence of Bryan's "Cross of Gold" and the pulpit eloquence of the Evangelical clergyman—perhaps Dr. Russell H. Conwell, in his celebrated Chautauqua lecture, "Acres of Diamonds"; then the traditional "elocution" and "declamation"—for which Lindsay's college, Hiram, was famed: the taste and skill, now probably extinct, for exhibitionistic virtuosity like that required, variously, for Byron's "Roll on, thou dark and deep" and Poe's "The Bells"; then simple forms of song, chant, and intonation such as are represented by the priest's plainsong responses in a *missa cantata* and by the traditional "cries" of street-vendors in London and New York. But Lindsay mixes, in his performance, oratorical effects with song and chant effects. This is the chief vice of his reading. His best poems start from strong rhythms, the dipodic rhythm of nursery rhymes, only with characteristic clusters of stresses

("Booth led boldly with his big bass drum");

and the oral "realization" ought, I think, to keep close to the tune: song-verse, not speech-verse, the semantic and expressive elements should adjust themselves to the drum-beat: the drums should dominate. But in "General Booth," Lindsay is beguiled by Protestant pulpit bathos into breaking up the rhythms in order to introduce sentimental pauses, accompanied by would-be touching, "melting" timbre, some kind of vibrato: "He saw . . . his *master*" (high quivering pitch on first syllable; then glide to low on second); "He saw—King Jesus." The rhythm ought to go banging, rattling, and jing-jing-jingling away without regard to these swell-pedal, vox humana luxuries.

Generally, I think, the speech parts of Lindsay's recordings are inferior to the song and chant parts; the reason is, probably, that, having once got past the barrier of chanting and singing (which he can do, with accurate pitch intervals), he is no longer self-conscious but, instead, anonymous—whereas when he undertakes to start the Chinese lady off on her last speech he gives her the potty, pseudo-cultivated tones of some Hokinson clubwoman asking to have read the minutes of the last meeting. Sheerly onomatopoeic effects and imitations, like the accelerating sequence of "boom-lay" in "The Congo,"—effects much used in the Sitwell and Walton *Facade*, a brilliant divertissement which must owe something to Lindsay,*—are not common: more characteristic are bold shifts of *pitch* from section to section: after the "shrill and high" tone of "Wild crapshooters, with a whoop and a call," the burden, the underlying *motif* of "Then I Saw the Congo," is chanted in a "deep rolling bass," that of some Russian or Negro *profondo;* then the voice goes into a lyric tenor. Lindsay uses something like two octaves in the range of his performances—though the intervals within the melodic sequences (*e.g.,* "Have you forgotten, deep in the ages,"—in "The Nightingale") are small,—a third, ordinarily, and the whole sequence confined to the pentatone. Of his three chief pieces, "The Nightingale" is the most elaborate in its oral devices,—the most calculatedly worked out—presumably because it far less obviously invites chanting than the others.

3

When one studies the text of Lindsay's poems, takes them seriously at their mythic level, one encounters the unresolved in Lindsay's imagination—the gap between his taste for drawing butterflies, ferns, and vines, and for "culture and refinement," and his genuine and creative taste for the vivid, the characteristic, the grotesque, the crudely vital.

The initial perception of "Booth Enters into Heaven" is admirable: Heaven centers, like any Mid-Western county seat, in "The mighty court-house square"; and the Judgment Day is imaged as it might well be in the mind of an American child, with Judge Jesus impressively coming to the Court-house to "review" the parade of the Salvation Army converts, all of whom, in a body, have accompanied the General as he marches into Heaven to be decorated—to receive his traditional "robe and crown." They march into Heaven just as they are—"saved," but characteristic: "vermin-eaten saints with mouldy breath," "bull-necked convicts," "loons with bazoos," banjo-banging lassies,—"the weasel-head, the snout, the jowl." Shall they remain so to all eternity? A difficult question to the religious imagination—that of personal identity and continuity in the after-life. Lindsay gets mixed up and off his intuitive balance. Compelled to think of Jesus as metamorphosing these Bowery characters, he indulges the strange fantasy (possibly

---

* *Facade* was first produced publicly at London, in 1923. Lindsay visited England in 1920; was hospitably received, and recited his poems, at London, Oxford, and Cambridge.

his own in untypical boyhood) of turning them into "classical" figures—"sages and sibyls now, and athletes clean" (doubtless some recall of Athenian youth discoursing with Socrates as well as of the Y. M. C. A. locker room.) However, then they should all be playing on (heavenly and classical) harps and lyres. But not so: now Lindsay swings back to his other, and happier, perception,— that the Salvationists should themselves stay fundamentally the same and so bring some much-needed warmth, color, and variety into Heaven.

> But their noise played havoc with the angel-choir . . .
> The banjos rattled, and the tambourines
> Jing-jing-jingled in the hands of queens!

The mythic structure of the more elaborate "Congo" is correspondingly more confused. The Negroes are said to have resented the piece as offering a genetic reduction, hauling them back to their origins. But, though Lindsay was not clear about what he was doing, he certainly did not mean to ridicule the Negro—even in the cakewalk of "Their Irrepressible High Spirits." And so far as he saw the ancestral African within (or behind) the American Negro, it was with considerable admiration and sympathy. His feelings, however, were very mixed—without his knowing it; hence the unintentional, the inartistic, ambivalence on which the poem founders. The confusion emerges most palpably in Section III, which corresponds to "Booth Enters Heaven." Is the "Hope" of the Negroes' "Religion" to be found in the Bible-banging, jubilee-revival religion of the opening episode, or is that Fundamentalist religion the Negroes' evil,—the survival of the witch-doctors and their menacing Mumbo-Jumbo? The Revivalist congregation shake the room with "Glory, glory, glory" and "Boom, boom, boom": doesn't this parallelism equate the two? Yet in quite another tone is the fanciful picture of a renovated Africa with the Twelve Apostles in coats of bright white steel mail sitting on their thrones (a translation of the Apostles into crusading Arthurian knights— certainly no archetypal image in the collective unconscious of the Negro, though it may have been a favorite fantasy of the boy Lindsay,) and the annexed fancy-picture of the cleaned-up Congo "slums,"—the tidied-up jungle—the work of "pioneer angels" interested in establishing a playground for "babes," while angels row up and down the Congo in blue boats. Is this progressive picnic, this Boy Scout campaign, a "revised version" of the revival religion, and that in turn of the worship of Mumbo-Jumbo; or does the fancy picture represent "true" (*i.e.*, liberal) religion, in which lies the Negroes' "Hope"?

The poem ends overtly or doctrinally, with the exorcism from Congoland of Mumbo-Jumbo; but only doctrinally—for the refrain recurs at the very end and would be felt by most audiences—and rightly, I think—to have a positive force.

Let us turn back to the first section, "Their Basic Savagery": Seeing the American Negroes, drunk, pounding on the tables and barrels, leads Lindsay into interpretation and evaluation.

> Then I had religion,
> Then I had a vision.
> I could not turn from their revel in derision.

"Had religion" must equal "got religion," *i.e.*, had a religious experience, was converted: viewing the meaning of the wine-barrel scene in terms of the African past, "I could not turn from their revel in derision." And Lindsay does not: even the cannibals' thirst for blood is sympathetically played down by the reminder of King Leopold of the Belgians and his cruel traffic in slaves. Or again: can there be anything very wicked about a battle-cry characterized as a "roaring, epic, ragtime tune,"—*i.e.*, the African archetype of "There'll be a hot time in the old town to-night"?

In the second section, the clusterings and oppositions are again impossible to make out with any assurance. What is the relation of the "wild crap shooters" and the juba dancers to the cakewalk of the rest of the section? The parallelism of structure between sections seems to require that after the return of the solemn refrain, "Then I saw the Congo," we have another glimpse back into archetypal Africa. But what follows the refrain, in section two, doesn't offer African fact but somebody's fancy—probably Lindsay's—of a future "Negro fairyland" along the "minstrel river" Congo—yet, strangely enough, a fairyland where menacing witch-men attempt to crush Negro gaiety by their "stern cold glare" and their warning of Mumbo-Jumbo's wrath against those who don't "walk with care." Where are our "values" here? The ascetic witch-men seem to have some alliance with prohibitions and commandments, prophets and clergy, morality and religion; yet it seems that we are to take the side of the "irrepressible high spirits" shown by the dancers. The section ends with as trick and evasive a solution as the third: the cakewalk dancers swing to the savage voodoo tune of "Boomlay," and the witch-men, apparently

—having been unsuccessful in frightening the gay out of their gaiety—join in—sing along with, "the scalawags prancing there."

4

I am not here attempting any complete discussion of Lindsay's poems. There are interesting pieces in other modes than the "Booth": the two surprisingly good epigraphic pieces, "Lincoln Walks at Midnight," and "The Leaden-Eyed"; the gay period *divertimento* of "Bryan"; the curious romantic lyrics called "I Walked Alone in the Jungles of Heaven" (originally "How Johnny Appleseed Walked Alone") and "I Heard Immanuel Singing." But they give one no perfection. The movement of American culture passes through Lindsay: his is a historic moment of participation; many lines pass through him and go on. He recognized the talent of his young fellow-townsman Robert Fitzgerald; he discovered the talent of Langston Hughes; he was a generous promoter of such contemporaries as Frost. He welcomed and encouraged Percy Grainger and Thomas Benton, "regionalists" and "folk-artists" in music and painting. But these are instances of his practical judgment as an "organizer": If one wants to feel what kind of poetic life flows through Lindsay, he can have the perception most efficiently through reading Lindsay's "Bryan" at its chronological position in Auden's *Oxford Book of Lighter Verse*,— a volume of poems largely anonymous, including

> Gay go up and gay go down
> To ring the bells of London town

and R. A. Millikan's witty version of eighteenth-century Dublin street-minstrelsy, "The Groves of Blarney."

The Idea of Great Poetry which hovers over us today is that of a mythic poetry which shall unite workmen and intellectuals by discovering in the shared, traditional tale its hidden, but not planted, import. Lindsay glimpsed the Idea. He had not, however, the intellectual vigor or subtlety requisite. What he can perform is unsteadily oscillatory between the romantic lyric (Poe, Swinburne) and anonymous folk-poetry. When he escapes from "bourgeois culture and refinement," it is by identification with the people and folk-art; but the escape is demanding, and he cannot then use folk-art as thematics for a mythic poetry. He expurgated some false refinements; he achieved a degree of poetic anonymity. He had faith in a unity of culture ahead of us.

Nils Erik Enkvist

The Folk Elements in
Vachel Lindsay's Poetry

Vachel Lindsay's debt to folklore and his use of folk materials and concepts are generally recognized. No systematic study of how he used and treated folk elements has, however, been made. This paper forms an attempt at outlining some of these elements in Lindsay's treatment of individual heroes and his analyses of the spirit of folk groups.

Lindsay's biography shows us that he did not restrict his intimate knowledge to one social stratum, but took part in the life of various segments of the population and learned to know different representatives of the American nation in their own surroundings. However, direct borrowing and use of folk items is not a characteristic of Lindsay's work. He had assimilated folk concepts to a degree where they colored his very philosophy and creative thought. Hence if we want to get at the influence of folk elements on Lindsay's poems we have to define them broadly as the unliterary trends, concepts, customs, art, or traditions of that part of the population with which he came into direct contact.

From *English Studies*, XXXII (December 1951), 241-49. Reprinted by permission of the Editor of *English Studies* and the author.

In his admiration of the pioneer Lindsay celebrated some typical representatives of the early Americans. Jonathan Chapman, alias Johnny Appleseed, is Lindsay's heroic paragon. A folk-tale character, a man of the people, possessing the supreme virtue of universal love and practising it in his daily life, Appleseed became a suitable embodiment of Lindsay's highest ideals. Just as Lindsay himself rambled about, spreading the gospel of beauty and art and hoping to leave a lasting imprint on the American mind, so Appleseed went west across the mountains on his self-imposed mission. The sources of Lindsay's knowledge of Appleseed were at least partly literary. The poet's object was, however, not to produce a detailed epic, but only to use Appleseed's character and a few main points of his life. Consequently, the most important of the Appleseed poems, *In Praise of Johnny Appleseed*, completely ignores the sordidness and disillusionment of the frontier migration. The poet's attitude is emotional, not historical or economic. This shifting of emphasis makes the treatment inconsistent: although Lindsay concedes that the participators in the westward current were ordinary mortals, no saints, he proceeds to stress the prophetic nature of Appleseed's deeds in the light of later events. In this way the hero's actions acquire purposefulness and he becomes a praiseworthy model instead of a poor vagrant suffering from an obsession.

Andrew Jackson, another representative of the pioneer generation, also receives his fair share of hero-worship in Lindsay's work, who never stopped to analyse the less ideal aspects of the Jacksonian regime. In spite of the fact that this very era gave birth to some of the evils of machine politics, he considers the popular enthusiasm of that period more than sufficient to counterbalance the evils. The Jacksonian period was a period of glory because it emphasized the importance of the pioneer in blue jeans, and because men in coon-skin caps then practised manly virtues. Lindsay's Jackson, therefore, is Old Hickory rather than the shrewd politician, a legendary folk-character and not a historical personality:

> Andrew Jackson was eight feet tall.
> His arm was a hickory limb and a maul.
> His sword was so long he dragged it on the ground.
> Every friend was an equal. Every foe was a hound.

While love and inherent goodness were the central characteristics of Appleseed, Americanism becomes the keynote of Lindsay's

Jackson-worship. There is only contempt for the enemy and for decadent Europe as personified by the 'British fops', only admiration of Jackson and his 'wild men, straight from the woods'. Thus the popular conception of Jackson offered the poet an opportunity to insist on the American tradition.

In the Springfield of Lindsay's youth the memories of Lincoln were still very strong. The great president suited our poet's general conception of the American hero: his origin was lowly, his ways and manners unsophisticated, he preserved the United States intact for future greatness and he helped to liberate the Negro. The most important of the Lincoln poems, *Abraham Lincoln Walks at Midnight*, shows us a simple, clear-cut popular figure:

> A bronzed, lank man! His suit of ancient black,
> A famous high top-hat and plain worn shawl
> Make him the quaint great figure that men love,
> The prairie lawyer, master of us all.

Again no detailed analysis is necessary. Lincoln is accepted in the character which was traditional among his most ardent admirers, a humble, unsophisticated, but admirable folk-hero who spent his life fighting for the people, an excellent example for future generations. In *Litany of the Heroes*, one of the key poems of Lindsay's hero-worship, Lincoln is the personification of ideal Americanism:

> Would I might rouse the Lincoln in you all
> That which is gendered in the wilderness,
> From lonely prairies and God's tenderness.

But while Jackson was described as swashbuckling Old Hickory, Lincoln is not subjected to a metamorphosis into Old Abe. Perhaps Lindsay found it possible to retain a serious, even a philosophical tone in the Lincoln poems, because the Lincoln tradition was closer to him and had not yet acquired the folk-tale character of the Jackson legend.

Lindsay's youth was the heyday of the Populist movement, and it is therefore logical that some of the Populist heroes were poetized as true representatives of the folk against the political machine. Governor Altgeld of Illinois was a German immigrant and Wm. J. Bryan, the presidential candidate in 1896, officially a Nebraska farmer; hence there was no doubt of their eligibility to Lindsay's heroes' gallery. His contact with these two gentlemen was of a more personal nature, for he had seen them both. Altgeld had lived in the Governor's Mansion at Springfield but a few blocks away from the poet's home, and Bryan had delivered speeches young Lindsay had heard. Here the poet had idols of flesh and blood, and their poetical treatment remains closer to the facts. *The Eagle that is Forgotten* is an elegy and shows Lindsay in a mood very different from his usual loud and robust force. *Bryan, Bryan, Bryan, Bryan* celebrates its hero as 'the one American poet who could sing outdoors', a person possessing some of the old pioneer virtues. Besides, Bryan as a politician was the representative of the venerable Jacksonian tradition in American politics. His outward appearance is again described in a characteristic way:

> In a coat like a deacon, in a black Stetson hat
> He scourged the elephant plutocrat.

At this point Lindsay's very language is penetrated by colloquial Americanisms: he sings the long-horns from Texas and the jayhawks from Kansas while commending the popular West and condemning Eastern capitalistic oppression. Thus even the contemporary heroes are conceived as the representatives of the folk and admired with a clear-cut, naive, subjective enthusiasm and with the usual lack of objective, historical reasoning. Nowhere does Lindsay stop to consider the intricate economic and financial problems that led to the failure of the Populist movement.

Theodore Roosevelt was another potent factor in the battle with capitalism. Because of his political convictions he was forgiven his aristocratic background and given a seat in the democratic rocking-chair:

> 'Great-Heart'! Roosevelt! Father of Men!
> He fed the children honey and bread.
> He taught them the ten commandments and prayer,
> Rocking there in his old rocking-chair,
> Or riding the storms of dream that he rode.

Roosevelt was a genuine 100% American, a professor both of pioneer virtues and pioneer faults, whose administration broke the golden age, and whose square deal and Roosevelt code were a sufficient basis for the revival of the original American spirit. Theodore Roosevelt was the ideal hero for a poet imbued with the American crusading zeal, and an aristocrat easy to transform into a folk-character.

Daniel Boone, Alexander Campbell, General William Booth, Mae Marsh, and many more are among Lindsay's heroes, but though their treatment is cordial enough, they are clearly subordinate characters when compared to the former. The poet did not attempt a description of their personalities, but used them as reference material for generalizations on virtue or the past, present and future of the United States. There is consistently more emotion than fact, and the most popular qualities get the loudest praise.

These instances suffice to show that in Lindsay's hero-worship 'folkliness' and goodness were identical. Many aristocrats of distant lands and times had excited his imagination ever since his youthful adventures among books telling him about heroic deeds of far-off times. Yet Lindsay never dethroned his heroes for Twain-ian scrutiny. For him, the mythological purity of King Arthur might well be employed as a suitable starting-point for appeals against white-slave traffic. However, as soon as the obvious facts of history begin to interfere with his consistent idealism, heroes like Alexander the Great or Napoleon become traitors of the human cause rather than admirable examples. Neither did far-off mythology ever incite Lindsay to his best. Where the ideals were close by in time or space, and thus familiar and tangible, his poems get the sweep and force of first-rate work. American history was the prime source he drew upon. These American figures were identified with the great western continent and its spirit, though the Americans of the pioneer era as well as those of Lindsay's day were a heterogeneous mass of individualists. However, instead of diluting his admiration into vague generalities, Lindsay adopted as poet the method of celebrating the American race, past and present, in the persons of those representatives he considered worthy of this supreme identification.

Actual American folklore gave Lindsay only one of his great heroes, Johnny Appleseed. The others were either historical personalities who had acquired some legendary qualities during intervening decades, such as Jackson and Lincoln, or later men and women of various occupations, who had contributed their share in promoting the physical or spiritual welfare of America. Even in the latter cases Lindsay proceeded to treat his heroes as folk characters. Where the historical facts did not suit his intentions, they were mercilessly discarded, and emotional evaluations used instead. These subjective analyses were performed on a 'folkly' basis. Lindsay can be said to have 'made folklore' out of history.

His imagination readily filled in the gap between reality and the ideal: he saw even his contemporary idols through magic spectacles which carried them back in time far enough for him to create new legends about them. These imaginary legends were what Lindsay built on. He was crusading for a greater and better America, and left his pseudo-folktales to be digested by posterity and assimilated into the mythology of the ideal American. His romantic mind tended to occupy itself with mystical concepts based on the ancient lore of various climes; perhaps his endeavors to provide his nation with a synthetic literary folklore were an attempt to compensate for the lack of a long-range historical perspective on American themes by applying folktale techniques to topical characters. By this device he at the same time succeeded in achieving originality and in freeing himself from alien traditions. Since there was a national American literary technique in the field of folklore, why not carry it over into the treatment of topical questions as well? In this sense Lindsay becomes the great modern balladmaker of American literature.

However, Lindsay was too didactic a poet to succumb to the characteristic folktale concept of fortuitous evil and good. The characterization of his major heroes is marked by a tendency to moralize and explain. In the case of Appleseed the moralizing takes the form of a scrutiny of the hero's achievements in the light of later events. The other heroes are celebrated in terms of their deeds or political creeds, and the motives behind Lindsay's choice of subjects are always clear beyond ambiguity. His characters are treated in a holistic folktale manner: they are either good or bad. But where a folktale would leave off, the poet begins his most enthusiastic praise on moral and ethical grounds. Lindsay was a man of strong creative talents, not a mere collector of folktales trying to give his audience metric versions of old materials. Yet his treatment of his heroes rests on a firm foundation of folk elements.

Lindsay was a descendant of men and women who had not been afraid to face the hazards of the pioneer West. He was brought up in an atmosphere where the deeds of the pioneers had acquired an aura of romantic glory. By the time of his boyhood the toils of the early settlers had made the United States a powerful country, whose progress seemed unthreatened by external powers. The darkest clouds on the American sky consisted of social evils, which then fashionable and current trends of thought interpreted as results of ever-increasing Eastern industrialization. It is against this background that Lindsay's interest in the pioneer should be focused.

The typical and representative pioneer is, however, an abstract myth with different literary manifestations. One cannot generalize on the basis of a heterogeneous class of rugged individualists. The middle-western farmer of 1900 was very different from the early pioneer, since even agriculture was rapidly turning into a capitalist enterprise. The southern mountaineers, often thought to constitute the nearest modern approach to the pioneer, were a class Lindsay did not consider worthy of direct identification with his ideal. Therefore he preferred to celebrate the pioneer generation in the person of some representative individual, rather than in direct and abstract terms.

However, Lindsay's Americanism was not limited to the past and he also recognizes the American present as a subject worthy of aesthetic treatment. In his scrutiny of his surroundings he found many of the best pioneer qualities very much alive, and so neon lights, movies and other innovations are included among his aesthetic properties. The movies especially were passing through a development unprecedented in the history of any art and were helping to create a standardized beauty understood by the middle and lowbrow majority of the people. For Lindsay the embodiment of this modern art was Mae Marsh, the motion picture actress he celebrated in a poem. The actor Edwin Booth, on the other hand, was a pioneer of Old World culture who played Hamlet in dreary barns on the prairies, where the barking of the coyotes mingled with the soliloquies of the prince. John Bunny also came in for an epitaph, being a member of Yorick's honorable guild, while Lucy Bates, a cabaret dancer on Broadway, was the modern representative of another time-honored art. Even the collegiate yell, which Lindsay considered the American equivalent of the Elizabethan sonnet, gives proof, to his mind, that America still is capable of a spontaneous folk art, though *The Kallyope Yell* is of more value as a poem than as a yell.

A feature surpassing even the motion picture in importance for today's American life is the automobile. In *The Santa Fé Trail* we have Lindsay's aesthetic tribute to the mechanization of vehicles. The main theme is the hectic rhythm of an endless number of cars passing by and symbolizing the life of 20th Century America and the spirit of progress. But the poem has a very tender undertone indicating that when the cars have passed, the supreme wonder still remains in Nature, and this cannot be surpassed by any man-made devices. It seems as though Lindsay would warn his contemporaries against an overvaluation of material success and material progress. Yet individual initiative and boundless American energy belong to the pioneer inheritance and are qualities to be praised. After giving the reader a synthesis of modern America and its spirit in *Billboards and Galleons* without even forgetting the funny-papers, Arrow shirts or their collars, his final prophecy remains one of transcending Americanism:

> Some day this old Broadway shall climb to the skies,
> As a ribbon of cloud on a soul-wind shall rise.
> And we shall be lifted rejoicing by night,
> Till we join with the planets who choir their delight.
> The signs in the street and the signs in the skies
> Shall make a new zodiac, guiding the wise,
> And Broadway make one with that marvellous stair
> That is climbed by the rainbow-clad spirits of prayer.

Lindsay's conception of the spirit of the American Negro has found a more detailed expression in his poems than has his treatment of any other American minority group. In *Adventures While Singing These Songs*, Lindsay's autobiographical foreword to the *Collected Poems*, he explains the sources of his knowledge of the Negro. The Southern background of both his parents accounted for the popularity of Negro songs and spirituals in his childhood home. Most of the time the Lindsays had at least one colored servant in the house, and further contacts took place all around him in his childhood environment. *The Congo* contains his great analysis of the Negro race. Lindsay was not an apologist for the colored people: he did not try to tone down those elements that can be considered African and to emphasize the characteristics added by their contact with American civilization. On the contrary, he exults in deriving the important characteristics of the spirit of the Negro directly from the savage jungle and introduces primitive parallels to the American environments that begin each section of the poem. The treatment of these elements affords an excellent example of the way in which Lindsay used familiar folk-material as a basis for his poetic imagination; the crap-shooting, the gambling and the revival meeting Lindsay must have been familiar with since childhood. *The Congo* is one of the poems that established Lindsay's reputation as a jazz-poet, but if *The Congo* is jazz, it certainly is not the jazz of polished floors and evening clothes but a poetical description of the rhythm of the unspoiled, unsophisticated Negro. In *Daniel* Lindsay adapts the tone of the spiritual to a Biblical theme. He anticipates *The Green Pastures* in his naive treatment of the subject according to the grotesque, but charming, colored tradition: the lions of Darius are just 'bad', Daniel was 'the chief hired man of the land', he 'stirred up the music in the palace band' and 'white-washed the cellar' and 'shoveled in the coal'. In *The Booker Washington Trilogy* we find a similar familiarity of epithets, which contributes to the vivid impression the poem makes, while *King Solomon and the Queen of Sheba* is less imitative of direct Negro elements, though its subtitle, 'A Poem Game', and the marginal notes bear witness to Lindsay's conception of the close relationship between dancing, acting, singing, and poetry. *How Samson Bore Away the Gates of Gaza* is again notable because of the colorful and imaginative language of 'A Negro Sermon'. Lines like 'Samson's heart was as big as a wagon' and 'O Lord look down from your chariot side' are strongly suggestive of the Negro spiritual, while finally *When Peter Jackson Preached in the Old Church* forms a brief description of a revival meeting, and is to be sung to a Negro spiritual melody. But there is more Negro influence in these poems than mere elements of thought and language. The repetition characteristic of most folk-art is adopted here for artistic effect, while the striking rhythm forms the common denominator of all of Lindsay's poems built on Negro elements, though it is not restricted to the Negro poems, but is found in *The Santa Fé Trail* and many other descriptions of modern American life.

The American Indian likewise excited Lindsay's imagination and poetic talent. The original inhabitant of the vast American continent naturally furnished him with a starting point for all his Americanism. Johnny Appleseed was loved by both Indian and White man and kissed both Indian and white children indiscriminately. In Lindsay's family, there seems to have been a tradition that there was an Indian somewhere in the ancestry. Lindsay was rather proud of this, pointing out that if there was one Indian in the family tree, there must be millions. To him the Indian race became a glorious yet abstract symbol for the vast spaces and endless prairies of early America, a symbol not to be overlooked in any description of pioneer society. The Indians of Lindsay's day lived on reservations; he could not be on familiar terms with them and his Indian is neither the heroic, admirable redskin of Cooper, nor Mark Twain's dissipated wretch. He is rather the historical predecessor of the white pioneer, who has a definite place in American history, and whose influence on the American past has become an influence on the American present as well. Hence the treatment is more romantic than realistic: the spirit of the Indian is identified with the original spirit of the American wilds and of the country Lindsay so deeply loved. In *Our Mother Pocahontas* the closeness to Nature in which the Indians lived is admired: Powhatan

> Was akin to wolf and bee,
> Brother of the hickory tree,
> Son of the red lightning stroke,
> And the lightning-shivered oak.

This Utopia, which he supposed characteristic of the every-day life of the Indian, was Lindsay's ideal. In this sense Pocahontas too was a part of the Nature in which she lived and her life was in many respects similar to that of the early pioneers: 'She traced the paths of Daniel Boone'. Hence American society should not be based on decadent European principles, but on the traditions of freedom, closeness to Nature, and lack of restraints, all traditions of the Indian. Thus Pocahontas is the mother of the American spirit:

> We here renounce our Saxon blood.
> Tomorrow's hopes, an April flood,
> Come roaring in. The newest race
> Is born of her resilient grace.

And this inheritance should mean more to every true American than any pride in Norse, Slavic or Celtic ancestry. *Doctor Mohawk* contains many autobiographical elements; Lindsay's country doctor father is no doubt the person alluded to and made into the epitome of America. But here too the American past includes the Indian as well as the white man, and the great Mohawk's example was set according to the best of the Indian tradition, which is the means of arriving at the final climax, a description of the 'uncaptured future' of the New World in terms of ancient Inca sun-worship. Similarly, in *The Tree of Laughing Bells* it is the Indian maid who makes the Wings of the Morning and tells the hero where to get the Laughing Bell. However, Lindsay's interest in the Indian was not purely aesthetic. He considered the neglect with which the Indians had been treated a shameful blot on American history, and in *The Hunting Dogs* the cause of the Indian race is openly declared one of his crusading objectives. His defense of the oppressed group, however, takes its most ardent form in *The Babbitt Jamboree*, where the fact that the Indian is no longer free is deplored as a serious breach in a tradition always endorsed by the United States, and which should be maintained in the future. He was an integral part of early American life and the symbol of a spirit worthy of admiration and preservation.

The other racial groups of the American population are not treated with equal ardor and knowledge in Lindsay's work. The poems on these minorities are further removed from the realms of folk concepts, and at the same time both more abstract and less forceful.

Although he did not have much use for decadent European society, Lindsay had a profound veneration for the ancient civilization and traditions of the Far East. In spite of the menial tasks performed in the service of an alien civilization, a San Francisco Chinese laundryman possesses qualities that can be acquired only through the slow process of assimilation of traditions handed down from generation to generation for thousands of years, and Lindsay's treatment of Chinese civilization shows him in a mood very different from that in which he sang the pioneer or the Negro. *The Chinese Nightingale* is both subtle and delicate, and lacks the loud force which is so typical of much of Lindsay's work. *Shantung* also proves Lindsay's interest in oriental lore, but it remains a poem about China and not about American Chinamen. Both these poems seem to infer that western culture is in many respects inferior to the oriental, which is founded on more peaceful and positive concepts, and that in the American synthesis there ought to be room for the best elements of the Chinese tradition.

Although the Gypsies share many of Lindsay's ideals, his treatment of them is clearly less enthusiastic than that of the Negro and the Indian. The open road, though free, is not equal to the virgin forest. The nostalgic longing for their own past made the Gypsies a melancholy race in Lindsay's eyes, a race lacking the robust characteristics of the Negro or the wild freedom of the Indian. The closest approach to the spirit of the Gypsy is in *I Know All This When Gipsy Fiddles Cry*. In *The Tramp's Refusal*, written 'on being asked by a beautiful Gypsy to join her group of strolling players', the Gypsies merely furnish a stimulating background for the poet's somber thoughts and self-criticism.

Lindsay approached the question of race on a basis which might be described as Jungian. In his opinion each race, each population group possessed a mass spirit of its own, which was predetermined by its past. Without stooping to a condemnation of any particular group he accepted the destiny of America as a synthesis of these elements. No tradition was too humble to be included: the African background of the Negro, the Oriental traditions of the Chinaman, the wild barbarism of the Indian were elements as valuable as the glorious pioneer tradition. Their fusion in a true spirit of universal love and understanding formed the rock on which Lindsay's optimistic Americanism was established.

William Rose Bénet

Twentieth-Century St. Francis

Not long ago I received a letter from Vachel Lindsay's sister, Olive Lindsay Wakefield, which with an accompanying poem by him, I take pleasure in printing here:

HOPE FOR THE BRAVE

Would I might wake St. Francis in you all,
Brother of birds and trees. God's Troubadour,
Blinded with weeping for the sad and poor;
Our wealth undone, all strict Franciscan men,
Come, let us chant the canticle again
Of mother earth and the enduring sun.
God make each soul the lonely leper's slave;
God make us saints and brave.*

It must be that Zofia Kossak's novel, "Blessed are the Meek," which makes St. Francis a living, breathing person for us, has

From *Saturday Review of Literature,* XXVIII (October 20, 1945), 47-49. Reprinted by permission of *Saturday Review.* Copyright 1945 by the Saturday Review Associates, Inc.
* Copyright by the Macmillan Company. "Collected Poems of Vachel Lindsay."

pointed out for me, as never before, Vachel Lindsay's resemblance to his own great hero, St. Francis of Assisi. Do you remember how Vachel's friends felt about those tramping adventures while "preaching the gospel of beauty"? It was the same affectionate tolerance and condescending appreciation which St. Francis's half-converted friends felt toward the young Bernardone and his travels through the world.

For many years now, I've thought of Vachel, not alone as my brother, my constant companion in college and confidential friend, but as the brother of all the world. For such indeed he was. He truly loved "all sorts and conditions of men," whether they were the miners of Ridgely, near Springfield, or the moonshiners of the Southern mountains or the Negro laborers who befriended him on his travels as he tramped through this America of ours, in the attempt to see it at first-hand, to find out for himself what our democracy is like.

A letter from our friend, Dean Willard Sperry, of the Harvard Divinity School, worded this characteristic of Vachel's so well that I must quote it. "Vachel's intense provincialism represents a maturity of thought which was very great. Only people who have strong local affection can be truly catholic and international." Vachel's introduction to his "Adventures While Preaching the Gospel of Beauty" puts the same thought another way. He wrote:

> The things most worth while are one's own hearth and neighborhood. We should make our home and neighborhood the most democratic, the most beautiful and the holiest in the world. The children now growing up should become devout gardeners or architects or park architects or teachers of dancing in the Greek spirit or musicians or novelists or poets or story writers or craftsmen or wood-carvers or dramatists or actors or singers. They should find their talent and nurse it industriously. They should believe in every possible application to art-theory of the thoughts of the Declaration of Independence and Lincoln's Gettysburg address. They should, if led by the spirit, wander over the whole nation in search of the secret of democratic beauty with their hearts at the same time filled to overflowing with the righteousness of God. Then they should come back to their own hearth and neighborhood and gather a little circle of their own sort of workers about them and strive to make the neighborhood and home more beautiful and democratic and holy with their special art. . . .

It was this which he labeled "The New Localism"; the heart of his "Gospel of Beauty"; which he carried about with him, and distributed through the farmlands of Missouri and Kansas on his last walking trip in 1912, just before he wrote "General William Booth Enters Into Heaven." Harriet Monroe and *Poetry*, a magazine of verse, hailed him then as an important new American poet. This small volume, the story of his experiences on that trip, Vachel himself considered his "central work." It was so he expressed it in a note to my husband, which he inscribed on the fly-leaf of a copy of the "Adventures While Preaching the Gospel of Beauty" during our never-to-be-forgotten Christmas season together in the old home, in December 1923. Here is part of what he wrote.

> 603 South Fifth Street
> Springfield, Illinois
> December 25, 1923

My dear Paul:

In many ways this will always be my central work. It records the trip to New Mexico—just before I caught the train at Wagon Mound and rode to Los Angeles (in the Pullman) and a little later in Los Angeles wrote "Booth."

It is the best possible commentary on all the poems in the "Booth" volume, because they were most of them from "Rhymes To Be Traded For Bread," and all of them written before "Booth" itself, like this book. People read this book only for adventure, but the proclamation and sermon are the important thing. . . . they map out my private life for a life-time, and in none of them is it hinted that recitation is to be my fate!

> With love,
> VACHEL.

In truth it did "map out" his private life, his aims and deepest hopes, for in 1929, when he returned to live in the home town, he did "gather a little circle" of his "own sort of workers" about him and strive to instill into them his ideas and dreams for making their neighborhood and home more "beautiful and democratic and holy." These were "the darlings of his heart," these were "the young." They, in turn, passed on their hopes and dreams for their city, to their fellows, to the next generation of high-school boys, who now are scattered throughout the world, still led by their dreams for a Golden Springfield and for a world where such dreams may have a chance to be carried out. Many of them dream in Vachel's own terms and use his very words. They recall, not just "The Congo" that captivated and thrilled them in high school; they soberly think of "The Leaden-Eyed" and "Factory Windows Are Always Broken." They think in terms of "The Net to Snare the Moonlight," of the time when every man in the world may possess his own small plot of ground, "a place of toil by daytime," and of "dreams when toil is done." Above all, they think of the building of that Springfield which *must* have "many Lincoln-hearted men" in order to "make a path of beauty clear between our riches and our liberty," where every citizen may "be rich toward God," and "Christ the beggar, teach divinity." They know too "A city is not builded in a day, and they must do their work and come and go, while countless generations pass away." Yet even this must not cause them to lose heart. Did not Vachel himself once warn them? "It takes three thousand years to make a California redwood, and it will take three thousand years to make an American city." Abraham Lincoln walks beside them in the jungle and speaks to them of the spirit dawn which yet *must* come, "the league of sober folk, the Workers' Earth, the shining hope of Europe free." As Vachel poured out in words his agony for the world, they now pour out their own in deeds, with the same desperate hope of helping to bring about the sort of world of which they dream—a world in which the rainbow flag of a united world government will be flying beside the nation standard in each capitol. Vachel had described this rainbow flag. He said it should be "a sewing together of all the flags of mankind; . . . with no regard for alliances or hostilities, but the flags arranged in alphabetical order or some such way. It would disturb few old loyalties while establishing a new one, introducing no new element except the idea of union." In such a fashion he made his own rainbow flag in 1918, by cutting up the flag page of the big dictionary. He pieced together, in one harmonious banner, a flag from each nation of the world and used it as his pennant glorifying the world state.

Was not this, in Shelley's words, "the trumpet of a prophecy"? Recently in that San Francisco where Vachel wrote of St. Francis, and found "what might be called the Franciscan soul of the Franciscan minority" in Professor and Mrs. E. Olan James across the Bay at Mills College—recently the greatest of World Conferences was held, a meeting of nations that would have gladdened his heart.

But the likeness of Vachel to St. Francis goes further. He had the truly Franciscan appreciation of all animate and inanimate nature. He loved "the souls of the tall corn," and the "gay little souls of the grass in the ground," as well as Rachel Jane with her enchanting song. Almost we can hear him talking to Brother Mouse and Sister Bee, and the Mysterious Cat, the chipmunk and

the grasshopper who is "the brownies' racehorse, the fairies' kanga-
roo," not to mention the king of yellow butterflies and his men,
the little turtle, so dear to all children, the two old crows, the
crickets who went on a strike, and the broncho who would not be
broken, whose death broke our hearts as well as Vachel's own. To
me the cries of the worms "beneath the daisy beds" as they cursed
the gardener in their black despair, and the ghosts of the buffaloes
racing in splendor through the night were most moving of all.
Once I asked Vachel about those earth worms whose story the
garden toad reported, whether it meant the children in the slums.
How scornfully he replied, "It means just what it says; don't try
to make something else of it!"—But I still think it is one of the
best of his social poems.

In contrast to all this, is his intense devotion to his home town,
the city of his "discontent," the city of visions, the city of "The
Golden Book" of his dreams. With a veritable heartbreaking affection, he brooded over his city almost as Christ wept over Jerusalem. Indeed he once wrote to his dear friend, Eleanor Dougherty,
Walter Hampden's sister, "No man consciously ever died for a
city. I wonder how that could be done. Sometimes I feel that I
could offer myself to the devil to be boiled alive, if only a beautiful
city could be made in exchange." . . . and in another letter he
wrote, "Like most all civilized people, you, Eleanor, must live on
art visible, rather than on art invisible, if you are to be satisfied.
I see so many dragons, demons and angels, that I do not need
Paris, to speak frankly. Speaking as an artist, I have no such thirst
ever. If I am alive enough to be thirsty, the angels bring me my
drink. I usually am not that much alive, and dodder around like
a June-bug, butting my head into nothing much. . . . I am under-
taking to teach other Springfield people to see the angels, demons
and dragons right here. . . . I have taken a vow to make this a city
of dreamers or die trying."

Here are excerpts from some of his other letters to Eleanor. You
may read them for yourself and see between the lines his spirit of
unity with all men, his love for those of every race, creed, and
color. The spirit is of St. Francis, but the words and phrases and
the subjects he discusses are of our twentieth century. One of my
young friends said of these letters of 1917 and 1918 "They are like
releases for tomorrow's newspaper. They fit into our thinking
today."

My dear Eleanor:
    This morning I mailed my second Photo-play article to *The*

New Republic. Then I began to answer a whole bushel of letters that have accumulated.

"The Birth of a Nation" passing through town, I went there tonight, and am almost converted to censorship. Why? Because the long battle with the censors has trimmed it into an infinitely more balanced and reasonable and artistic production than it was when I took Percy MacKaye to see it in New York two years ago. It really isn't so bad, even from a Northern standpoint now. And, by omission, it is more decent to the colored folks and the abolitionists. . . . It is still Thomas Dixonish, but hasn't his pronounced yellow streak. . . . At best, this film assumed that some people have a *right* to sit still, while others bring their food to them. . . . Mumbo Jumbo hoo-dooed the South in an infinite number of subtle ways and the poison is far more perverting than any Southerner realizes to this day. . . . The longer I live the more I am for Old John Brown, and if you ever hear of me being burned alive, it will be because I insisted on mounting the pyre with some Black who had not trial by jury. As long as white men are not burned alive without trial, black men should not be. . . . "The Birth of a Nation" is better than it was, but I am still for Old John Brown.

April 4, 1917.

My dear Eleanor:

There does not seem to me one chance in a hundred that you will get this letter. [Eleanor was in France helping as a volunteer nurse. O.L.W.] I take it for granted that the mermaids will get it. But I want to write to you tonight, even if there is little chance of your getting the letter or of your reading it with any great interest if it does get to you.

My heart is very sad tonight about the war. I have not the heart to challenge Wilson. I voted for him and cannot regret it—yet Jane Addams's dauntless fight for peace goes home to my soul. I feel with her—and with him—and am all torn inside. Certainly I have no sympathy with the fire-eaters. It is so easy to get killed for a cause—but it is a bitter thing to think of killing other people. I would a hundred times rather get killed than kill anybody. . . . I feel as guilty as if I had done it all tonight—or had a hand in it.

No man knows where the thing will end. The world may be starting on its French Revolution—and may not stop seething till everything has been turned over three times. . . . Certainly I hate war with all my soul. I would like to make a bargain with the devil and be crucified a hundred years, and thus abolish it, instead of going out and shooting up my fellow man—not so very certain I am abolishing anything. When I took my first big walk, I had conversations with old Southern soldiers who had been through all this. I suppose men went through it in King David's time.

Isn't it amusing that Springfield, the wettest city in the United States, voted itself dry yesterday? . . . If this town can go dry, it can do a lot of other impossible things.

Even if this letter goes to the bottom of the ocean, I am glad to have written it. I suppose I will always have the big circle of friends, and when it comes to the final intimacies, tread the wine-press alone. Who cares how the inner watch ticks, so it keeps time? I lean to the dim ghost of you and make my vague confessions, and feel the better for it. . . . The world turns over and over, and you are writing letters to many soldiers at the front you do not know, like a good nurse and Christian. Well, the thought of such a person is a comfort. You have done a deal for me just by doing that.

With all proper nonsense,
NICHOLAS VACHEL LINDSAY.

October 12, 1918.

My dear Eleanor:

I find myself writing two letters to your one. . . . My pen is as impatient as your feet. So here, at quarter of twelve, Saturday night, after a really hard week's work, when I am unable to look at one more page of the "Golden Book," I still must soothe myself with a letter. It is like dancing after brick laying, though I have never done either.

The third edition of the German peace acceptance was on the street half an hour ago. . . . I find strange thoughts in me, on war and peace. I wonder if I am self-deceived. But it seems to me this is not the last chance good men all over the world will have to fight. Anything that lifts me out of the sheer mystical non-resistance that pacificism means in the face of the universe, persuades me to the next war. The ironical book, "Germany and the Next War," flashes before me as a warning. Yet the latter part of the "Golden Book" might be called, "America and the Next War," and I see my mind moves in the same channel, once I consent in my soul, to be a soldier in any exigency,—and I have consented long ago—and would have been in the ranks today if this book had not seemed my first duty. And now I am so deep in the book, my mind is one hundred years ahead most all my waking hours, and often this war looks as far back as the Civil War. There has been, in spite of my one-hundred-year trance, a certain pressure from friends, so that it seemed almost unknightly to stay out, when so many were dying in the world's last crusade.

But I begin to see that this "world's last crusade" idea is an illusion. . . . "We won't come back till it's over, over there" is a rash promise. This is not my last chance to die, nor my last chance for martyrdom. I must have faith in life, and its unfolding, and finish my book and keep my nerve. I am quite sure that inside of five years, there will be crusades as risky as the present war, if not so popular, where a man may use his dead body as a vote on the side he chooses for the right. Personally I would rather die for the "poor nigger" than any other breed of man. It is easier to be martyred for France, than for a "nigger"; but I suspect I will have my chance in one of two other ways.

First, after the world government is formed, it will have to have an army pretty active in some quarter of the world, and perhaps an army as big as the present Allied forces, in some sudden secession exigency. But I think the more probable chance for me will come in some little row where strikers are being shot down. In such a case, I do not think I would quibble. I would be with the fool strikers, right or wrong. Sometimes I live like a Tory, I grow more Tory every day, but God grant I do not die that way. It would be like dying an infidel, or a blasphemer. I want a clean Christian death. Yet I see a possible thing to defend that may look Tory to half the radicals of the world,—the world government of which Wilson will likely be President. Though he lets Debs go to jail, yet I am for him, for he is a radical by comparison with the Mikado and the Kaiser, and I think they both will go down if his world government is firmly established. And it will be the first foundation of world order, worth all our blood.

The last two-thirds of my book puts the great war for the defense of the World Constitution against Secessionists, one hundred years hence. I am not sure it will wait that long. In my book I do everything I can to inculcate loyalty to the World flag, the flag of such a world Constitution as Wilson stands for. Since I commit myself to it in my book, I must be prepared to make every sacrifice for such a flag, if once it is set flying. So, this is my thought of death. Today is not my last chance to die or to suffer the limit of agony. Both are inevitable with mortal man. I must simply do my work and go forward. VACHEL.

John T. Flanagan

Vachel Lindsay: An Appraisal

There can be no question that the reputation of Vachel Lindsay has declined sharply since the days when he won fame as a bardic poet and recited "The Congo" to thousands of tense listeners. When Norman Foerster published the first edition of his popular anthology *American Poetry and Prose* in 1925, he naturally included Lindsay and selected six poems to represent one of the freshest American talents since Poe. A quarter of a century later, F. O. Matthiessen in *The Oxford Book of American Verse* allotted Lindsay twenty-one pages and chose to include six poems. But in 1965 the situation was quite different. In their anthology entitled *American Poetry*, Gay Wilson Allen, Walter B. Rideout, and James K. Robinson resurrected Frederick Tuckerman, gave space to H.D., and allocated forty pages to many obscure and untested poets such as Robert Creeley and Wendell Berry, but failed to include a single poem by Vachel Lindsay. The nadir of Lindsay's fame has certainly been reached when a collection of American verse running in excess of twelve hundred pages completely omits his work.

From *Essays on American Literature in Honor of Jay B. Hubbell,* ed. Clarence Gohdes (Durham, N.C.: Duke University Press, 1967), pp. 273-81. Reprinted by permission of Duke University Press.

This abrupt shift in critical esteem of a poet who once enjoyed international recognition can hardly be unexpected. In an age of abrasive sound, of deliberate harshness and shock, Lindsay's often musical lines seem to find small appeal. In an age of intellectual poetry when thought seems to transcend form or is even consciously muddy in the hope that it will impress readers as profound, Lindsay's ideas seem vague and naïve. In an age of dissidence and revolt, when nonconformity in both action and thought becomes freakish, Lindsay's romanticism is jejune. In an age of ringing asseveration of civil rights and human dignities, Lindsay's patriotism seems parochial, a pallid imitation of Whitman's grander sympathies which is clearly out of joint with the times. Even Lindsay's symbolism, his frequent use of the butterfly and the spider, of the rose and the lotus, appears obvious and commonplace at a time when symbols are extremely complex and personal.

Contemporary poets have their causes and are sometimes annoyingly insistent in pleading them. It is not only the hirsute folksingers who argue in verse for Marxist proletarianism or desegregationism. But Lindsay also had causes for which he crusaded —temperance, a mild agrarianism, municipal beautification, the replacement of the Mammon-soul of avarice in public life with the spirit of beauty. The trouble is that in comparison these goals seem naïve and elusive. Today's partisans of a militant church will hardly be much impressed by the dream of a world religion in which Springfield, Illinois, would become the site of a great cathedral open to all and adorned by statues of Gautama Buddha, St. Francis of Assisi, and Johnny Appleseed. The Village Improvement Parade, symbols and lines from which decorate the end pages of Lindsay's *Collected Poems*, seems as ineffectual and pointless now as the miscellany of sketches and proclamations which once filled his "annual" periodical, the *Village Magazine*. Lindsay was unquestionably sincere, but many of his esoteric visions carried little conviction to his readers. As he once wrote in his journal, "I scarcely think one thought a year, and visions come in cataracts."

Indeed a chief factor accounting for Lindsay's decline in popularity is the illusionary character of much of his thinking. He had a rich and colorful imagination but virtually no sense of logic. Stephen Graham, the English writer who accompanied Lindsay on a hiking trip through the Rockies, observed that his companion "loves oratory more than reason, and impulse more than thought." Edgar Lee Masters, his first important biographer and an acquaintance of the poet, expressed it differently; according to him, Lindsay's religion made him "myopic to reality." It should be remembered that the poet's mother, a dominant personality and an orthodox Campbellite, often thought of her son as a great Christian cartoonist. Egyptian hieroglyphics, first garnered from a close study of Rawlinson's history of Egypt, adorn his drawings, and the Orient was never far from his fancy. His sister Olive had married a medical missionary and had lived for some time in China; by sending him pictures of the Kamakura Buddha and other sculptures she provided another channel of images for the poet. Lindsay's interest in the graphic arts, his reading in art periodicals, his vicarious experience of exotic countries—all inflamed his imagination without giving substance or firmness to his own work. As Masters pointed out, Lindsay with all his interest in drawing was never able to sketch the human face.

Any appraisal of Lindsay must of necessity take into account his deep nationalism. He was proud of being an American and once wrote in "Doctor Mohawk": "The soul of the U.S.A.: that is my life-quest." It pleased him to think of an Indian strain somewhere in his remote lineage and to remember that his mother could possibly claim some Spanish blood. Even greater than his profound Americanism was his pride in his Southern ancestry. "No drop of my blood from north/Of Mason and Dixon's line," he wrote in his tribute to Alexander Campbell. His "Litany of the Heroes" introduces Lincoln and in the final stanza equates Woodrow Wilson and Socrates as martyrs to a cause, the one figuratively and the other literally drinking a cup of hemlock. A late poem, entitled "The Virginians Are Coming Again," utilizing the title as a refrain, pours scorn on the Babbitts of the world he knew with their avarice and their rackets and cites Washington, Jefferson, and Lee as exemplars of a different code. The statue of Old Andrew Jackson striding his charger and bearing a sword "so long he dragged it on the ground" became a symbol to the poet of native power and glory.

Lincoln of course received his sincerest accolade and in Springfield, Illinois, Lincoln's town, Lindsay was born and died. The poet visualized the tall gaunt figure, still wearing his shawl and his top hat, pacing restlessly near the old court house, unable to sleep because the world was sick. For Lincoln the poet retained a lasting devotion. But Lindsay found American heroes elsewhere and often in strange locations. He imagined himself on a mining camp street in California listening to Edwin Booth as the actor enunciated a "whispering silvery line" which he was resolved to speak aright. He praised Governor Altgeld of Illinois, savior of the Chicago anarchists, as "the eagle that is forgotten." He could celebrate John L. Sullivan, the strong boy of Boston, who "fought seventy-five red rounds with Jake Kilrain." William Jennings Bryan, of course, won his admiration, and in the poem with the quadruplicate title he praised the "gigantic troubadour" who "scourged the elephant plutocrats/With barbed wire from the Platte." Bryan's defeat for the presidency Lindsay saw as a plot engineered by Mark Hanna in which Western democracy collapsed before the onslaught of Wall Street and State Street.

And always Johnny Appleseed fixed his attention, the gentle Swedenborgian horticulturist who came down the Ohio River with a cargo of tracts and apple seeds determined to distribute both along the frontier. Johnny Appleseed was the man who "ran with the rabbit and slept with the stream" and who as a knotted and gnarled septuagenarian still planted trees in the clearings of Ohio and Indiana. Once Lindsay even imagined his saintly pomologist as praying on Going-to-the-Sun Mountain in Glacier Park surrounded by a flood of dark rich apples.

For a time Lindsay was the victim of his own success. Harriet Monroe printed his early poems in *Poetry: A Magazine of Verse*; and H. L. Mencken some of his later ones in the *American Mercury*. But he won fame on the recital platform, in a thousand churches, schools, auditoriums, lecture halls—declaiming, shouting, whispering as his lines ebbed and flowed, providing his own acoustical accompaniment, his own clarion and tympani. Inevitably the spell faded and the fountain dried up. Lindsay could and did write better verse than "The Congo" but audiences demanded "The Congo" just as concert-goers demanded the C sharp minor "Prelude" from Rachmaninov. In a letter to his friend Lawrence Conrad he referred to the poems on General Booth and the Congo with positive disgust. "I have *had* to recite those two poems and those only, since 1913, till I have nearly cracked up the back." Lindsay lost his touch even when he tried to write in the same vein. Later poems like "The Trial of the Dead Cleopatra" reveal both the poet's orientalism and his lush fancy but lack the magic of "The Chinese Nightingale." In the late 1920's, as many letters confirm, Lindsay grew physically tired and emotionally frustrated. Also, according to the latest biographical dicta, he was a victim of epilepsy. It is small wonder that he eventually chose the path trod earlier by Hart Crane and later by Ernest Hemingway,

becoming one of the three great American literary suicides of the
twentieth century.

Early in his life, perhaps when he was peddling "The Cup of
Paint" and "We Who Are Playing" along New York's Broadway,
selling his poetic leaflets for two cents, Lindsay resolved to write
brassy, stentorian verse, verse suitable for oral delivery and immediately challenging to his audiences. He even devised a label for it,
the "higher vaudeville." Generations of listeners became familiar
with these fortissimo poems, rich in alliteration, heavy of accent,
full of spondaic feet and emphatic caesuras. Transposed to the
printed page, they carried elaborate stage directions. "John Brown"
he envisaged as a classical antiphony, with a leader and a chorus
alternating, the leader providing the substance of the poem, the
chorus or audience interrupting with leading questions: *What
did you see in Palestine?*" "Daniel" was intended to combine
touches of "Dixie" and "Alexander's Ragtime Band." "The Santa-
Fé Trail" was to be sung or read at times with great speed,
preferably in a rolling bass, the interpreter was advised to utter
the resonant place names of the second section like a union depot
train-caller, but to enunciate the synonyms for auto horns with a
"snapping explosiveness" and finally to end with "a languorous
whisper." Carl Van Doren pointed out years ago many of the
ingredients of Lindsay's poetic style: the revival hymn, the sailor's
chantey, the military march, the Negro cakewalk, even fragments
of patriotic songs. The result of this mélange, as seen conspicuously
in "The Congo," "General William Booth Enters into Heaven,"
and "The Santa-Fé Trail," became Lindsay's trademark and one
of the most distinctive achievements in the whole range of American poetry. Even in the booming verses so familiar to audiences
there are memorable phrases or lines, but chiefly they linger in
the memory because of their stridency.

What readers and critics of Lindsay's work often overlook today
is the poet's gentler side, his attention to little things, his softness,
his tender romanticism, which led Masters to term "The Beggar's
Valentine" one of the "most moving love poems in the language."
The subject matter of these briefer poems is in itself revealing.
Lindsay could write about mice, turtles, snails, crickets, toads,
grasshoppers, crows, butterflies, and meadowlarks. The dandelion
as well as the rose and the lotus appealed to him, and memories of
long hours of toil in the wheat fields under a blazing sun could not
erase the pleasure in being in the open air, as a reading of
"Kansas" will confirm. Some of the larger mammals also attracted

his attention, the buffalo of the prairies and the golden whales of California, although inevitably these creatures became symbolic. He remembered the experience of watching hands on a Western ranch attempting to discipline a young horse, and he later transmuted this experience into "The Broncho That Would Not Be Broken." These poems are brief, whimsical, sometimes wryly humorous, though in general humor was not Lindsay's forte. There is probably no better example of the poet's delicate touch than "What the Rattlesnake Said":

> The moon's a little prairie-dog,
> He shivers through the night.
> He sits upon his hill and cries
> For fear that *I* will bite.

Here the sly anthropomorphism, the simple language, the use of the familiar ballad stanza in an unpretentious lyric—all suggest Lindsay's deftness.

As a love poet Lindsay was generally less successful. He seemed unable to get away from triteness and conventional hyperbole. Early poems to unknown inamoratas are hardly memorable. "With a Rose, to Brunhilde" was addressed to Olivia Roberts, a Springfield neighbor and writer who attracted him briefly. Sara Teasdale, to whom he dedicated his *Collected Poems*, was his Gloriana, but although he exaggerated her physical qualities (her "burning golden eyes" and her "snowy throat"), his romantic admiration for her never achieved impressive form. Briefly he thought that a girl he had met while he was teaching at Gulfport Junior College in Mississippi, Elizabeth Wills, was his Dulcinea, but although he compared her to a bird's wing which "spreads above my sky," his devotion was not transformed into imperishable verse and his offer of marriage was spurned. After his marriage in 1925 to Elizabeth Conner he published a number of love poems, collected in *The Candle in the Cabin* and suffused with a romantic color, but this "weaving together of script and singing," as the subtitle has it, is not particularly successful. Most of the poems reflect the Glacier Park scenes which the couple viewed on their honeymoon, and even the landscape descriptions are curiously subdued and flat.

The subjects which moved Lindsay most deeply were places and people intimately associated with his own early life, or subjects with which he could achieve a family and almost a racial intimacy. "The Proud Farmer," a quietly impressive tribute to his maternal grandfather E. S. Frazee which in tone and workmanship reminds

one of Masters's tribute to his own grandmother, "Lucinda Mat-
lock," is genuine and devoted. The Hoosier preacher-farmer who
read by night and built his world by day left an indelible mark
on both his daughter and his grandson and became the subject of
one of Lindsay's best elegies. "Dr. Mohawk," the account of a half-
mythical figure who is both the poet's putative aboriginal ancestor
and his physician father, suggests the son's fear of and respect for
his parent and Dr. Lindsay's understandable bewilderment at the
occasional behavior of his gifted son. "Billboards and Galleons,"
inscribed to Stephen Graham, is a fantasy inspired by his days at
Biloxi and contains the reference to Don Ivan, his Spanish ancestor, whom Lindsay conceived as a friend of Columbus and a guest
of Queen Isabella.

Lindsay's natal town of Springfield, even though he spent many
years away from it, always cast a spell on him. His hope for the
future of the community was unrealistic but genuine. "A city is
not builded in a day," he declared and added that a great city need
not be large; neither Athens nor Florence achieved immensity.
What was needed most was "many Lincoln-hearted men." He
certainly envisaged the Village Improvement Parade as taking
place in Springfield and hoped that farm boys, builders, craftsmen,
marchers of all kinds carrying banners inscribed with slogans
would bring about a municipal revolution. But even though the
slogans might win approval ("Bad public taste is mob law—good
public taste is democracy"), the parade in Springfield or anywhere
else never got started. To his chagrin Springfield remained the
city of his discontent.

Of a different nature were the tributes paid to public figures, the
well-known encomiums to Jackson, Lincoln, Altgeld, Bryan, Alexander Campbell, Governor Bob Taylor of Tennessee, sincere if not
always highly perceptive, terse characterizations which seized upon
familiar details and phrased them memorably. Lindsay attempted
no career judgment but sought rather a brief illumination, a vision
of light or a brilliant profile, and often achieved more than pages
of expository prose could do.

Some of his most striking effects occur in poems less familiar
than "The Congo" or "The Santa-Fé Trail" although he employed
identical methods. "Simon Legree—A Negro Sermon," the first
part of the Booker T. Washington trilogy, is a fanciful account of
a meeting between the ignominious overseer and the Devil in Hell
where each tries to outdo the other in viciousness. Legree's puffed-
out cheeks which were a fish-belly white in color probably owe

something to Mark Twain's description of Huck's father but are not necessarily less vivid because of the similarity, and the picture we are given of the overseer gambling, eating, and drinking with the Devil on his wide green throne is one of Lindsay's magnificent achievements. Equally vivid is "The Ghost of the Buffaloes" with its extraordinary picture of the animals stampeding madly,

> Stamping flint feet, flashing moon eyes,
> Pompous and owlish, shaggy and wise.

One remembers, too, the parade of fabulous animals invoked in "Bryan, Bryan, Bryan, Bryan," the bungaroo and giassicus, the rakaboor and hellangone, all mixed up with prairie dog and horned toad and longhorn. In a very different key is the poem "I Know All This When Gipsy Fiddles Cry" in which his own experiences on the open road, begging and tramping in a way that Whitman never did, breed a sympathy in him for those wanderers who for centuries have been itinerant without losing their identity or their interest.

The critics have not always been kind to Lindsay, although he has had his defenders. Conrad Aiken, writing in *Scepticisms* in 1919, was willing to credit the poet with originality but objected to the orotund style, the echolalia, the banalities. He also found fault with Lindsay for being overly topical, thus denying him the very virtue celebrated by others of making use of the American scene in a frank and unhackneyed manner. Aiken gave Lindsay small chance for survival unless he abandoned the traits which inhere basically in the higher vaudeville. Llewellyn Jones was less harsh, but he also preferred the quieter poems. Yet he felt that some of Lindsay's tributes might well be grouped together into a kind of American hagiography. T. K. Whipple in *Spokesmen* asserted categorically that Lindsay was the author of *six* poems, the chosen six including of course all the famous bravura pieces plus "The Chinese Nightingale." Writing in 1928, only three years before the poet's death, Whipple could say, "His achievement has not yet been commensurate with his possibilities." Stephen Graham in a kind of obituary letter alluded to Lindsay's bitter disillusionment in love and to his deliberating grief at the time his mother died; he also termed Lindsay the greatest American poet of his age. Willard Thorp wrote in the *Literary History of the United States* that the twenty or so of Lindsay's poems which the poet's audiences clamored to hear over and over again "are as exciting as when they were first declaimed." William Rose Benét was convinced that Lindsay's best work would be read with admiration by posterity at the very time that he as the editor of an important literary periodical was constrained to refuse the poet's latest productions.

Ludwig Lewisohn, William Marion Reedy, and Carl Van Doren all thought highly of Lindsay's gifts although none was willing to deny obvious imperfections. In *Many Minds* Van Doren pointed out Lindsay's limited range but praised him for his free use of the American language, for his willingness to introduce a new idiom into poetic practice. Edgar Lee Masters cited nine poems as being among the poet's best, added another twenty as being significant, and concluded that collectively these poems constituted "the most considerable body of imaginative lyricism that any American has produced." To offset this enthusiasm one might allude to Allen Tate's cautious assertion that Lindsay's early poems had an original rhythm but that his use of language was undistinguished and his poetic subjects on the whole rather dull. Horace Gregory and Marya Zaturenska in their *History of American Poetry* quote liberally and approvingly from Lindsay, although they discourage anyone from reading through the *Collected Poems* and feel that some of the verse would not have been allowed to stand if Lindsay himself had been a more reliable self-critic. It is interesting that they found "I Heard Immanuel Singing"—a poem which Lindsay himself treasured—a valuable and interesting American spiritual.

In one of the last poems of the late Theodore Roethke, entitled "Supper with Lindsay," the author imagined Lindsay stepping into his chamber carrying the moon under his arm and deluging the furniture with a flood of creamy light. The two poets ate a meal of homely food together—corn bread, cold roast beef, and ice cream—until the lunar glow began to fade. With that change Lindsay decided that the feast was over and rose to depart, asking as he did so to be remembered to William Carlos Williams and Robert Frost. Of the three names Lindsay's in his time was the best known, as celebrated as a platform performer and declaimer as the Russian poet Andrei Voznesensky is today. Lindsay's verse has earned him a permanent place in American literature, and future anthologists who deny him that place will reflect only their own myopic vision.